A Straightforward Guide to

THE RIGHTS AND OBLIGATIONS OF LEASEHOLDERS AND FREEHOLDERS

Roger Sproston BA MSc

Straightforward Guides
www.straightforwardbooks.co.uk

Straightforward Guides

© Straightforward Co Ltd 2024

All rights reserved. No part of this publication may be reproduced, in a retrieval system, or transmitted by any means, electronic or mechanical photocopying or otherwise without the prior permission of the copyright holder.

978-1-80236-348-7

Printed and bound by 4edge www.4edge.co.uk

Cover design by BW Studio Derby

Whilst every effort has been taken to ensure that the information in this book is correct at the time of going to press, the publisher and the author accept no responsibility for any errors or omissions contained within.

CONTENTS

Introduction

SECTION 1

Chapter 1
Changes to Leasehold Law and Practice to 2024 — 15

The Leasehold Reform (and Ground Rent) Act 2022 — 15

The Leasehold and Freehold Reform Act 2024 — 18

The Building Safety Act 2022 and the Fire Safety Act 2021 — 22

Amendments to the Landlord and Tenant Act 1985 — 25

Change to planning rules in 2021 — 30

SECTION 2

Chapter 2
The lease. What it is and how it works — 35

Freehold, Commonhold and leasehold. — 35

Leases and tenancies — 36

Different types of leasehold property — 37

The right to buy — 39

Shared ownership — 40

Head leases and sub leases — 41

**

SECTION 3

Chapter 3
Respective obligations of leaseholders and freeholders   45

Obligations of leaseholders   47
Onerous conditions   47
Blanket conditions   49
Access   50
Obligations of freeholders   51
Exclusive possession and quiet enjoyment   51
The section 48 notice   52
Good management   53
Assignment of leases   56
Breach of lease   57

SECTION 4

Chapter 4
Service charges and the law   63

General   63
What goes into a service charge?   65
Unreasonable service charges   66
The First-Tier Tribunal   68
Service charge demands   71
Sample service charge demand   72

Consultation with leaseholders	77
Major works and long-term agreements	77
Landlords statement of why works are necessary	78
Estimates	78
Notification to leaseholders	78
Consultation	78
Freeholders' response	79
Other protection for leaseholders	80
Grant aided works	80
Late charging	80
Pre-charging	80
Court costs	81
Service charges held on trust	82
Insurance	83
Period of grace	84
The role of a recognised tenants association	84
Statements of accounts to leaseholders	85
Challenging service charges	86
Right to require information	86
Challenging the reasonableness of service charges	89
Forfeiture for unpaid service charges	90
Exceptionally high service charges	91
Ground rent demands-sample demand	95

SECTION 5

Chapter 5

The new provisions 0f the 2024 Leasehold and Freehold Reform Act	99
Purchase of the freehold and extension of the lease	99
Enfranchising or extending leases-the current law	101
Leasehold Reform, Housing and Urban Development Act 1993	102
The Collective Right to enfranchise-What is it?	103
How do I prepare for a claim?	104
The individual right to extend leases-What is it?	111
Enfranchisement – refusal	115
Enfranchisement of Houses	119
Landlord and Tenant Act 1987: First Refusal	123

SECTION 6

Ch. 6. The formation of a Flat Management Company 133

What is the purpose of a company set up to manage flats?	134
The management company	134
Transferring ownership of the freehold to the new company	137
Appointment of officers	137

Insurance considerations	140
Maintenance and repairs	140
Banking	142
Rent and service charge collection	143
Preparation of annual budgets	143
Maintenance of accounting records	144
Keeping flat owners informed	145
Directors' meetings	145
Shareholders meetings	146
Model service charge/fire safety budget	149
Model service charge accounts	151
Glossary	153
Index	159
Useful addresses	163

****

INTRODUCTION

Over the last 50 years or so, the law covering leasehold property has developed in a manner that has given more and more protection to leaseholders. This protection was seen as necessary because all too often leaseholders have been victims of poor management by (often) unscrupulous landlords, particularly around service charge delivery and management of service charge accounts.

In the public sector, there has been, in the past, a marked lack of knowledge and resultant management problems, particularly around service charges.

Since the 1960's, laws have been introduced designed to provide a regulatory framework for the dealings between freeholder and leaseholder, initially concerning the acquisition of the freehold of properties, by leaseholders, and in the 1980's around the provision of service charges and overall management. The 1985 Landlord and Tenant Act, as amended by the 1987 Landlord and Tenant Act, and the 2002 Commonhold and Leasehold Reform Act provide for a series of steps which landlords must observe when spending service charge money of leaseholders in their blocks. Further changes to the Landlord and Tenant Act have been introduced as a result of the Building Safety Act 2022 and the Fire Safety Act 2021, discussed in Chapter 1.

It is surprising how many freeholders and leaseholders live in ignorance of their rights and obligations, even though such a significant body of legislation exists to protect those rights. In 1993, the Leasehold Reform and Urban Development Act extended those rights initially granted in the 1967 Leasehold Reform Act to the purchase of the freehold and extension of leases. Collectively, leaseholders can purchase the freehold of a block (enfranchisement) and individually leaseholders can extend their leases by a given number of years past its existing life. These steps are clear but can be problematic and are described in full in this book.

In May 2002, the Government introduced the Commonhold and Leasehold Reform Act, which introduced new legislation protecting leaseholders amending the 1993 Leasehold Reform Act. This Act introduces the 'no fault' right to manage where, subject to certain criteria leaseholders can take over the running of their flats, without having to prove fault. A new form of ownership was also introduced, 'commonhold'.

The First Tier (Property Chamber) Tribunal, which came into effect in July 2013, following the The Transfer of Tribunal Functions Order 2013 oversees disputes and other issues between leaseholders and freeholders.

The general principles covering the setting up of a flat management company, and how to run a company effectively, are also outlined. This is a natural follow on to the acquisition of the freehold of a block, whether by enfranchisement or voluntary sale.

One area worth mentioning is that of the scandal concerning high ground rents, increasing at a rate which eventually makes a leasehold property un-saleable. Big developers, such as Taylor Wimpey, and many others build the properties, then sell off the freehold for a high price to companies who then exploit leaseholders both with rising service charges and escalating increases in ground rent. The ongoing clamour for change has resulted in the implementation of both the Leasehold Reform (and Ground Rent) Act which came into force on June 30th, 2022, and The Leasehold and Freehold Reform Act 2024. This latter Act has fallen short of what campaigners have asked for over the years but nevertheless goes someway to bolster leaseholders' rights.

Both Acts are covered in chapter 1, along with various other recently introduced Acts.

Grenfell Tower and the cladding scandal

Another major area that has arisen since the tragic Grenfell Tower fire in 2017 is that of building safety. There is now a new body of law concerning the safety of buildings, particularly fire safety which affects both leaseholders and building owners. The Fire Safety Act was passed into law in May 2021 and has significant consequences. This will be explained, along with the other changes to the leasehold landscape in Chapter 1.

Overall, the book is designed to raise the awareness of leaseholders who wish to understand what a complex relationship between landlord and tenant often is and also to help landlords understand their own obligations.

****

SECTION ONE

CHANGES TO LEASEHOLD LAW AND PRACTICE TO 2024

Chapter 1

Changes to Leasehold Law and Practice to 2024

The Leasehold Reform (and Ground rent) Act 2022
The much talked about and eagerly anticipated Leasehold Reform (and Ground Rent) Act came into force on June 30th, 2022, except for retirement properties where it will not come into force before 1 April 2023.

What does the 2022 leasehold reform legislation change?
The Act makes the following changes to laws relating to leasehold properties.

Ground Rents capped to a 'peppercorn' (£nil):
Ground rents on 'Regulated Leases' will be capped at a 'peppercorn' (£nil). Material fines may be imposed on freeholders attempting to charge leaseholders ground rents in relation to a regulated lease.

Will 2022 leasehold reform apply to all leases?
2022 leasehold reform will affect 'Regulated Leases'. These are leases granted after the date the legislation came into force

(commencement date), as well as leases entered into before the commencement date, but which are surrendered and re-granted after this date.

Leasehold reform will not apply to 'Excepted Leases', these including where:
- The lease expressly permits the operation of a business, not including a home business within the meaning of Part 2 of the Landlord and Tenant Act 1954 (see section 43ZA of that Act).
- The freeholder is a community land trust.
- The leasehold property is within a building controlled by a co-operative society.
- The lease is a home finance plan lease, including where a rent to buy finance arrangement is in place (this should not be confused with a shared ownership lease – see below for more information on shared ownership leases and leasehold reform).

Leasehold reform 2022 and shared ownership leases
Shared ownership leases will be impacted by the Act. Shared ownership leases will be considered 'Regulated Leases'. Ground Rent will be capped at a peppercorn (£nil) for shared ownership leases entered into after the commencement date, in respect of the share of the property owned by the leaseholder. Leaseholders are not liable for any Ground Rent

that may apply under the lease to that share of the property which they do not own and so, under this proposed legislation, shared ownership leaseholders will have their Ground Rent capped at a peppercorn (£nil).

As mentioned above, leasehold reform coming into force on June 30th, 2022, will not be retrospective in its effect. Therefore, those who have entered into a shared ownership lease prior to the new legislation coming into force will continue to have to pay a Ground Rent (if their lease requires) following these 2022 changes to leasehold law.

Ground rents following non-statutory lease extensions
Following the Leasehold Reform (and Ground Rent) Act becoming law, will still be possible for leaseholders to extend their lease via the non-statutory lease extension process. This process simply involves coming to an agreement with the freeholder, with advice and representation from a lease extension solicitor.

Where a leaseholder pursues a non-statutory lease extension, the freeholder will still be able to charge a ground rent under the new (extended) lease, but there are the following restrictions:
- Ground rent can only be charged up to the end date of the current lease term. No ground rent can be charged in relation to the extended period.

- The ground rent charged up to the end date of the current lease can be no more than the ground rent stipulated by the existing lease.

The Leasehold and Freehold Reform Act 2024

The Leasehold and Freehold Reform Act 2024 received Royal Assent on Friday 24 May on the last day of the so-called 'wash up' period before the UK's general election. However, most of the provisions will not come into force without secondary legislation, probably in 2025/6.

The Act, which affects property in England and Wales, was the very last bill passed in the 'wash up'. This is the period following a call for a general election during which parliament rushes some agreed bills through the legislative process to avoid losing progress made and abandons others, for example, the Renters Reform Bill has fallen.

The Act was then published on 3 June 2024 but as stated, most provisions in the Act will come into force later. Other key areas of the Act are regulation of remedies for rent-charge arrears, recovery of legal costs etc. through service charge, repeal of Section 125 of the Building Safety Act and Section 118 – higher risk and relevant buildings: notifications in connection with insolvency.

What is absent from the Act is the plan to phase out ground rent for existing leaseholders or cap it at £250 a year as had been suggested by Michael Gove. Dealing with the issue of existing ground rents will be an item for the next government.

The Act strengthens existing consumer rights for homeowners and introduces new ones. It introduces fundamental changes to the valuation methodology and legal process with a view to making it cheaper, easier, fairer, and more transparent for leaseholders to extend their leases and buy their freeholds. The key provisions of the Act include:

- Longer lease terms. Leaseholders can now extend their leases by an additional 990 years with ground rent reduced to a nominal 'peppercorn' rent, removing the need for leaseholders to extend their leases more than once.
- The Act introduces a majority ban on leasehold houses, with only a very limited category of permitted leasehold houses allowed outlined in the Act.
- The abolition of marriage value will reduce the premium payable significantly for leases of less than 80 years. Marriage value is the increase in the value of the property following the completion of the lease extension, reflecting the additional market value of the longer lease.
- The Act also removes the two-year ownership requirement for extending leases or purchasing the

freehold, allowing new leaseholders to act immediately.

- Mixed-use buildings may now qualify to buy their freeholds and the right to manage (RTM) increasing the commercial property element from 25% to 50% of floor area to allow a building to qualify for enfranchisement or RTM.

Freeholders will now be required to pay their own costs except in low-value claims and can now be forced to retain any non-participant flats or commercial leases in collective enfranchisement claims.

The Secretary of State is to prescribe the deferment and capitalization rates required to allow the new formula in the Act to work. They would be set at market rates, to be reviewed by regulation every five to ten years. These rates will be set by way of secondary legislation by the new government in due course.

Importantly, until secondary legislation is in place to implement the key provisions of the Act, there is still uncertainty about when, if ever, the provisions of the Act will come into effect. There will be a delay and depending upon who the Secretary of State and government of the day turns out to be. It should also be remembered that one parliament cannot bind its successors, so it would also be open for any future government to pass further primary legislation amending or repealing the Act in whole or in part, depending upon the new government's priorities and commitments. So, it is still very much a watch this space to see what the new government decides to do.

Building and Fire Safety
Owing to various serious developments relating to flatted blocks, in the main the Grenfell Towers tragedy of 2017 and bad practice perpetrated by building companies and solicitors relating to the practice of fixing high ground rents which increase as time goes on, thereby trapping leaseholders who subsequently find it very difficult to sell their homes, numerous changes have been introduced which have affected leaseholders, freeholders and managers.

Although these changes are, overall, positive developments, in particular building and fire safety, some of the outcomes will cost leaseholders more in charges, particularly associated fire safety charges.

Below, I have outlined the main areas of change.

The Fire Safety Act 2021
The Fire Safety Act 2021 applies to England and Wales and amends the Fire Safety Order 2005 ("the 2005 Order"), and along with the Building Safety Act 2021 is part of a collection

of legislation that aims to tackle the recommendations within the Grenfell Tower Inquiry.

The legislation clarifies that for any building containing two or more sets of domestic premises:

- The 2005 Order applies to the building's structure and external walls and any common parts, and applies to the entrance doors to individual flats opening into common parts; and
- References to external walls in the 2005 Order include "doors or windows in those walls" and "anything attached to the exterior of those walls (including balconies)."

The aim of these amendments to the 2005 Order is to clarify that the **Responsible Person** (owner of the premises such as. the freeholder or agent) must manage and reduce the risk of fire for these areas. The fire risk assessment will therefore be required to cover these areas. The clarification empowers the local fire and rescue authority to take enforcement action in respect of these areas.

Although the Government is providing funding to landlords to reimburse costs for replacement cladding works, charging for other fire safety works (particularly waking watch) has raised a number of questions and challenges for landlords and leaseholders.

Waking watch

Waking watch is a fire safety system where suitably trained staff continually patrol the floors and the exterior perimeter of a building to maintain the safety of its occupants from fire. The aim of a waking watch is to ensure there is sufficient warning in the event of a fire to support the evacuation strategy.

A waking watch is required when the presence of dangerous cladding or fire safety issues changes the evacuation policy of a building from stay put to simultaneous evacuation. This change requires fire marshals to patrol the building 24 hours a day looking for signs of fire. The provision of waking watch has left leaseholders facing average costs of £17,897 per building, which equates to £331 per flat).

The new Waking Watch Relief Fund will pay for the installation of fire alarm systems in high-rise buildings with cladding, and remove or reduce the need for interim safety measures such as a 'waking watch'.

Some buildings have already installed fire alarm systems due to the significant savings they offer, with leaseholders in those buildings expected to collectively save over £3 million per month.

Fire reports-What fire report do you need?

The government issued new advice in response to the Grenfell fire in 2017. Building owners must ensure that blocks of any height are safe. Mortgage lenders require a report, for which fire engineers cut holes in buildings to check wall systems. Fewer than 500 engineers have indemnity insurance for this. Cladding and insulation samples are tested to check they match the building's design. If any are combustible the system is deemed safe if a three-storey replica wall passes a fire test. The cost is split between all flat owners in the block. The Royal Institution of Chartered Surveyors, the Building Societies Association and UK Finance have launched an External wall system form (EWS1). valid for five years (see below). The need to obtain this report has led to problems obtaining mortgages and buying and selling generally. Many leaseholders have suddenly found themselves trapped in their properties, unable to sell.

Where do you get the report?

Flat owners can't commission the report because they don't own the building and can't give permission for holes to be cut. Leaseholders should ask their building's managing agent for the EWS1 and latest fire-risk assessment. There is no legal obligation to provide this report but, if your agent declines, consider asking your MP to intervene as it is essential that you can get a copy of the report.

Don't wait until you need to remortgage or sell your flat. Ensure that your building's freehold or agent has found a surveyor to sign your EWS1.

What if walls are found unsafe?

The new guidance affects buildings with any flammable cladding or insulation, not only the type that was on Grenfell Tower. Building owners must check that fire breaks are correctly fitted inside walls. In 98 per cent of cases where surveyors have removed cladding to inspect this, they have found defects.

Amendments to the Landlord and Tenant Act 1985

The Buildings Safety Act 2022 (which has itself been amended by the 2024 Leasehold and Freehold Reform Act 2024, notably repeal of section 125 and section 118 coming into effect from July 24th 2024) introduces new provisions, Sections 17A to 17X, into the Landlord and Tenant Act 1985 (the "1985 Act"). Readers will probably be familiar with Sections 18 to 30 of the 1985 Act which set out the legal framework for variable service charges. The Act sets out detailed provisions, but also provides for the Secretary of

State to introduce Regulations which will set out additional obligations and detail in the future.

The key features of Sections 17A to 17X are:

The charges will be referred to as "Building safety charges" and will cover the accountable person's building safety costs. "Building safety costs" are defined as the costs or estimated costs incurred or to be incurred by, or on behalf of, an accountable person for a higher-risk building in connection with the person carrying out prescribed building safety measures that will be required under the Act.

They apply to:
- "higher risk buildings" - this term is yet to be defined but is expected to include residential buildings of 18m or more in height, or over six storeys, or student accommodation.
- "long leases" over 21 years, including shared ownership leases.

If leases do not include provisions that impose an obligation on the landlord to carry out the necessary works, a right of access for those works and/or an obligation on the leaseholder to pay for those works, these provisions will be implied into the lease. Landlords can make demands every 3 months and leaseholders will have an obligation to pay within 28 days of the landlord's demand for payment. The provisions in the lease regarding apportionment of service charge costs will also apply to the building safety charges: if none, an application can be made to the First-tier Tribunal (Property Chamber) for determination.

Building safety charges will operate separately from variable service charges and are excluded from the definition of variable service charges. However, many elements of that regime are repeated within these new Sections:

- The charges, the costs, and the work undertaken must be reasonable.
- The accountable person will have to undertake consultation (inevitably to be called "Section 17K consultation") when entering a qualifying long-term agreement or undertaking qualifying works. The Act provides for Regulations to be passed here: these will no doubt mirror the Section 20 consultation process, but perhaps provide an opportunity to review the threshold amounts in both cases (which has been discussed for Section 20 for a number of years), and hopefully better reflect modern procurement practices. The accountable person can apply for dispensation from the requirements.

The 18-month rule:

Costs must be charged to leaseholders within 18 months of being incurred, except in cases where they have been served a notice about the amount to be charged.

Service of a summary of tenants' rights and obligations with demands for payment.

The two regimes will differ in the following ways:
- The Section 17K consultation requirements will not apply in urgent cases: this is an exemption and will not require an application and order for dispensation in such circumstances. However, landlords (or the accountable person if different) will have to provide an exemption notice: there will be a prescribed form of notice published in due course.
- Landlords (or the accountable person) must provide budget and accounting period information to leaseholders. Failure to do so gives leaseholders a right to withhold payments.
- There must be a reconciliation of actual versus estimated amounts within 28 days of the end of the accounting period. This is a much tighter timeframe than the 6-month period landlords operate generally operate for service charges.

- The charges must be held in a designated account (or accounts) and on trust for the building safety works. Leaseholders have a right of inspection of the account information. The Act does not exclude registered providers from the need to operate designated accounts in the same way it does for service charges.
- Landlords will have to take reasonable steps to take any available financial support available for these works and not be able to charge residents for costs covered by such financial support. Although the principle of no double-recovery of costs (i.e. by not charging leaseholders where grant funding has been received) has been established in service charge case law, the provisions impose a new mandatory obligation on landlords to apply for any funding support available.

There is also a new obligation of co-operation where there are multiple parties involved in the building and delivering these services: this helpfully recognises more complicated developments that can involve intermediate leases and/or managing agents.

The First-tier Tribunal (Property Chamber) will have jurisdiction to determine applications about who must pay building safety charges, the amounts, the date of payment and the manner in which it is payable. The County Court will have jurisdiction over the new implied obligations.

Although these proposals are likely to be tweaked and supplemented by the detail in the Regulations that will follow, landlords should start to consider how they set up their systems and processes ready for this new type of charge that will sit alongside service charges. Leaseholders should be fully aware of these charges.

Changes to planning rules in 2021

From August 1, 2021, planning rules fast-tracked adding two extra storeys of flats on top of blocks with three to eight floors, built between 1948 and 2018. The permitted development right (PDR) applies to would create up to 800 new flats a year, government analysis shows. There are also implications for leaseholders, who could lose about £9,000 each in inconvenience and reduced value, reckons the Leasehold Knowledge Partnership (LKP):

www.leaseholdknowledge.com

But you stand to lose far more if your block qualifies for the PDR: regardless of whether flats get built, the fact it could happen pushes up the development value of the freehold. According to LKP,1.2 million flats would have to pay between

£12,000 and £29,000 more to buy their freeholds – or convert to commonhold, if that became law.

****

SECTION TWO

THE LEASE, WHAT IT IS AND HOW IT WORKS

Ch.2

The Lease-What it is and How it Works

Freehold, Commonhold and Leasehold

The strongest form of title to land is that of freeholder. Freehold title lasts forever; it may be bought and sold or passed on by inheritance. Freeholders can use their land for other purposes. They may also, if they wish, allow other people to use their land, usually through a lease or tenancy.

A lease grants the leaseholder permission to use the land for a certain period, which can be anything from a day to several thousand years. It will usually attach conditions, for example, that the leaseholder must pay rent (usually a sum of money-refer to the introduction concerning underhand practices in this area). The lease may, but does not have to, put certain restrictions on what the leaseholder may do with the land. But it must, in order to be a lease rather than merely a licence, grant the leaseholder 'exclusive possession'. This is the right to exclude other people, especially the landlord, from the land. Such a right need not be absolute, and exceptions to it are explained later in the book: but it is enough to give the leaseholder a high degree of control over the land, which has become, for the duration of the lease, very much the leaseholder's land rather than the freeholder's.

A lease, unless it contains a stipulation to the contrary, may be bought, sold, or inherited; if this happens, all the rights and duties under it pass to the new owner.

A new form of ownership, that of commonhold, was introduced by the Commonhold and Leasehold Reform Act 2002. Commonhold means that the purchaser of a flat in a block will own the flat in which they live, much the same as the leaseholder but will have no lease as such. They own their property in perpetuity along with common ownership and an obligation with other commonholders, to maintain the common parts. Although this book is concerned mainly with the rights of the leaseholder, most of the issues will concern the commonholder, as they deal with the maintenance of common parts.

Leases and Tenancies

Confusion is often caused by the fact that, although the terms leaseholder (or lessee) and tenant are legally interchangeable, they tend to be used in different senses. The tendency is to refer to short leases as tenancies: the more substantial the rights conferred, and the longer the period for which they run, the more likely it is that the agreement will be referred to as a lease. It is common for private landlords to insist on prepayment of rent or a deposit before granting a tenancy, and almost all landlords will levy a service charge to cover the cost of some activities that are peripheral to the central one of providing housing; but despite these costs it would be true to say that the principal financial responsibility accepted by a periodic or short-term tenant is that of paying the rent.

The position of a leaseholder is very different. The major financial commitment will usually be a substantial initial payment either to the landlord (if the lease is newly created) or to the previous leaseholder. This is normally done through a mortgage. There is still a rent, as mentioned earlier, called a ground rent, payable to the landlord. The leaseholder is only liable, under the provisions of the 2002 Commonhold and Leasehold Reform Act, to pay ground rent on receipt of a demand from the landlord.

Different types of Leasehold Property

The great majority of leases relate to flats rather than houses. As also mentioned, the government has banned the sale of most leasehold new build houses. Where flats are sold, each purchaser acquires a lease that gives them specified rights over the parcel of land on which the flats stand. These rights, of course, are shared by the leaseholders of the other flats. In addition, however, each leaseholder gains the right to exclusive possession of part of the building occupying the land - his own flat. The freehold of flatted property will often be retained by the developer, although increasingly it will be sold to a property company. Formerly, it was common practice for the freehold to be retained even when separate houses were built. This allowed the freeholder to retain an interest in the property and, above all, to regain full possession of it when the lease expired. However, the position of freeholders has been weakened by two several key pieces of legislation, the Leasehold Reform Act 1967 the Leasehold Reform, Housing and Urban Development Act 1993, and the Commonhold and Leasehold Reform Act 2002. Their overall effect is to entitle leaseholders either to the freehold of houses or to a new lease of flats. In view of the legislation, there is now little point in the original owner attempting to retain the freehold of land on which houses have been built. The exception is where a house is sold based on shared ownership - see below.

Most residential leasehold property therefore consists of flats. Of these, most are in the private sector, comprising purpose-built blocks and (especially in London) conversions of what were once large single houses. The freehold will usually belong to the developer, to a property company, or sometimes to the original owner of the site. House leases, where they exist, normally give most of the repairing responsibility to the leaseholder - services provided by the freeholder, and therefore service charges, are minimal.

In flats, however, although the leaseholder will normally be responsible for the interior of the flat, the freeholder will maintain the fabric of the building and will recoup the costs of doing so by levying service charges on the leaseholders. This is an area of potential conflict between leaseholders and freeholders and is discussed further on in the book.

The right to buy

The general shift from renting to owning meant that sometimes flats have been sold in blocks that were originally developed for letting to tenants: the result is often a 'mixed tenure' block, with both leaseholders and tenants. Although this sometimes happens in the private sector, it is particularly common in blocks owned by local authorities and housing associations, for it is to these that the statutory right to buy applies. This right was created by the Housing Act 1980 and allows local authority tenants, and some housing association tenants, to buy their homes at a heavily discounted price. Tenants of houses are normally sold the freehold, but tenants of flats become leaseholders. A similar but less generous scheme has been introduced covering many housing association tenants not already qualifying for the full right to buy.

Purchasing a council home has been, for most that have done so, a very satisfactory investment. A minority of purchasers have, however, met with serious difficulties, particularly where they have become leaseholders in mixed tenure blocks of flats. Chapter four looks at some of the problems affecting management and service charges.

Shared ownership

Another result of the trend towards home ownership was the dramatic expansion of shared ownership. Currently, purchasers of shared ownership property have the same problems as purchasers of other property, lack of mortgage opportunities. Shared ownership is a form of tenure that combines leasing and renting. However, the term 'shared ownership' is something of a misnomer because ownership is not, in fact, shared between the leaseholder and the freeholder. The lease relates to the whole property, not part of it, and the shared owner is as entitled as any other leaseholder to consider himself the owner of his house.

The key point about shared ownership leases is not that they give an inferior form of tenure to other leases but that they have different conditions attached. The leaseholder pays less than the full value of the lease; typically, half. In exchange for this concession, he/she pays not the normal notional ground rent but a much more substantial rent. However, a shared owner is much more a leaseholder than a tenant, and, like other leaseholders (but unlike tenants) is responsible for the internal repair of the property and, in the case of houses, usually the fabric of the building too.

Shared owners usually have the right to increase their stake as and when they can afford it: this is called 'staircasing' because the owner's share goes up in steps. If the property is a house, the freehold will normally be transferred when the owner's share reaches 100%, and they will then be in the same position as any other freehold homeowner. If it is a flat, they will continue to be a leaseholder but there will no longer be a rental (other than ground rent).

Head Leases and Subleases

It is the right of the leaseholder, unless the lease specifically forbids it, to sublet the property, or part of it, to someone else. This means that the leaseholder has delegated some of his rights over the property to another person. Obviously, he cannot delegate rights greater than his own, and he cannot grant a sublease of the whole of his rights because this would leave him with no interest in the property: it would, in fact, amount to the same as an assignment. So, it is necessary for a sublease that the original leaseholder be left with something; either some period of time or some part of the property.

SECTION THREE

RESPECTIVE OBLIGATIONS OF THE LEASEHOLDER AND FREEHOLDER

Ch. 3

Respective Obligations of Freeholders and Leaseholders

For centuries the law did little to regulate the relationship between freeholders and leaseholders. The view was taken that they had entered into the relationship of their own free will, and it was up to them to agree whatever terms and conditions they liked.

In the twentieth and twenty first century, however, the view has grown up that some types of bargain are inherently unfair and even those that are not may still be open to exploitation.

An example of the first type is an agreement that residential property will revert to the original freeholder at the end of a long lease. This meant that when 99-year leases expired, leaseholders found that their homes had abruptly returned to the outright ownership of the heir of the original freeholder, leaving them as mere trespassers liable to be ejected at any time. In practice, freeholders were usually willing to grant a fresh lease, but sometimes only at a very high price that the leaseholder might well be unable to afford. In some cases, freeholders insisted on reclaiming the property however much the leaseholder offered, and the law supported them. This is the state of affairs that led to legislation entitling almost all residential leaseholders to extend their leases, and many of them to claim the freehold. As mentioned, the Leaseholders and Freeholders Reform Act 2024 entitles, or will entitle, those who extend their leases to do so for 999 years.

The freeholder's right to demand a service charge is an example of an arrangement that is fair in principle but open to abuse in practice. It is inevitable, especially in flats that responsibility for some types of repair cannot be ascribed to any individual leaseholder and must therefore be retained by the freeholder; who must, in turn, recoup the cost from leaseholders. However, some freeholders abused this system by levying extravagant service charges that made the charge a source of profit. To prevent this, there is now a substantial body of legislation designed to ensure that freeholders carry out only the works that are necessary and that they recover their legitimate costs and no more. The complicated rules governing this are chiefly found in the Landlord and Tenant Act 1985 (as amended) the Housing Act 1996 and the 2002 Commonhold and Leasehold Reform Act. These are described in Chapter Three. Also, as outlined in chapter one, there are now additional charges introduced into the Landlord and Tenant Act 1985, namely charges arising out of the Building Safety Act 2022 and the Fire Safety Act 2021. Under the Landlord and Tenant Act 1987, either party to a long lease (one originally granted for at least 21 years) may go to court (or a First Tier Tribunal) to argue that the lease is deficient in some way and needs to be changed. If only the one lease is affected, the court could vary it. Sometimes, however, a number of leases may need to be changed; in this case either the freeholder or 75% of the leaseholders may apply.

Where the law is silent, however, it remains the case that the lease can contain any covenants or conditions that the freeholder can induce the leaseholder to accept.

Obligations of Leaseholders

Leases have been drawn up at different times and vary depending on prevailing legal practice and on the chief concerns of the freeholder at the time. However, similar terms are found in typical leases.

a: Onerous conditions

This is a term applied to conditions that have the effect of seriously reducing the value of the lease. Such a condition is not necessarily an unreasonable one; it may serve some legitimate purpose. But no one should sign a lease containing them without fully understanding their likely effect.

A common example of an onerous term is a restriction on the kind of person to whom the lease may be sold (or 'assigned' - see below). For example, a housing scheme may have been intended specifically for the elderly. Clearly, it could not be maintained as such if leaseholders were free to assign or bequeath their leases to whomever they please, so the lease will say that it may be assigned only to persons above a certain age, and that if it is inherited by anyone outside the age group it must be sold on to someone qualified to hold it. Although this could be described as an onerous term because it makes it more difficult to find a buyer and may reduce the lease's value, it is reasonable given the need to ensure that the scheme continues to house elderly people exclusively. And the restriction it imposes is not too severe because so many potential purchasers qualify.

However, some leases define much more narrowly to whom they may be sold. Sometimes the freeholder is a body owned and run by the leaseholders themselves, and in these cases, it is usual to require that all leaseholders must join the organisation and, if they leave it, must immediately dispose of the lease to someone that is willing to join. Again, such a term is not necessarily unacceptable. If the organisation makes relatively light demands on its members (perhaps no more than a modest admission fee or annual subscription), the restriction is unlikely greatly to diminish the value of the lease. If, however, the organisation expects much more from its members - perhaps that they actively take part in running it, or that they pay a large annual subscription - the value of the lease will be severely reduced because it will be difficult to find purchasers willing to accept the conditions. A key point is whether the organisation has power to expel members, thus forcing them to sell; and, if so, in what circumstances and by whom this power can be exercised.

b: Blanket conditions

Slightly different from the onerous condition is the blanket condition. It is common for leases to contain sweeping provisions that would, if they were enforced, give the freeholder considerable control over the leaseholder's life.

For example:
- *Pets* Leases often lay down that the leaseholder may not own pets or may not do so without the freeholder's permission.
- *Business Leases* often lay down that the leaseholder must not run any sort of business from his home.
- *Use as residence.* A lease will generally say that the property is to be used for residential purposes and will

sometimes attempt to restrict how many people may live there apart from the leaseholder.

It is easy to see why freeholders want such clauses in the lease. But the kind of blanket rules that appear in many leases go too far. A rule against any pets at all forbids not only noisy dogs but also inoffensive pets such as a budgie or a goldfish. In the same way, prohibiting business activities means that the leaseholder may not use his home to write a book for publication, or address envelopes, and so on - types of home working that could not possibly inconvenience anyone.

The reality is that this kind of provision is seldom enforced. Freeholders, and their lawyers, like it because they feel that it preserves their freedom of action, allowing them to decide whether to enforce the lease if it is clear that one of these blanket conditions is being broken.

c: Access

Virtually any lease will contain a clause allowing the freeholder to enter the property in order to inspect or repair it. This has the effect of qualifying the leaseholder's right of exclusive possession (see below), but only subject to certain conditions. The freeholder (or the freeholder's servants, such as agents or contractors) may enter only at reasonable times, and subject to the giving of reasonable notice. If these conditions are not met, the leaseholder is under no obligation to allow them in; and, even when the conditions are met, the landlord will be trespassing if he enters the property without the leaseholder's consent. If the leaseholder refuses consent even though the time is reasonable and reasonable notice has been given, the landlord's remedy is to get a court order against the leaseholder compelling him to grant entry. It is probable, in such a case, that the landlord will seek, and get, an award of legal costs against the leaseholder.

Obligations of Freeholders
Exclusive possession and quiet enjoyment
The first and most important obligation on the freeholder, without which there would be no legal lease at all, is to respect the leaseholder's rights of 'exclusive possession' and 'quiet enjoyment'. Exclusive possession is the right to occupy the property and exclude others from it, especially the freeholder. Quiet enjoyment is another way of underlining the leaseholder's rights over the property: it means that the freeholder may not interfere with the leaseholder's use of the property provided that the terms of the lease are observed.

However, the leaseholder's right to quiet enjoyment applies only to breaches by the freeholder or the freeholder's servants such as agents or contractors. It is important to note this because the term is sometimes thought to mean that the freeholder must protect the leaseholder against any activity by anyone that interferes with his use of the property: this is not so. For example, if the freeholder carries out some activity elsewhere in the building that interferes with the leaseholder, the leaseholder's right to quiet enjoyment has been breached and he is entitled to redress unless the freeholder can show that the activity was necessary, for instance to comply with repairing obligations under the lease. But if the interference is caused by someone else, perhaps another leaseholder, the freeholder's obligation to provide quiet enjoyment has not been breached. And it is worth stressing in this connection that even if the other leaseholder is in breach of his lease, it is entirely up to the freeholder whether or not to take action: other leaseholders have no power to force the freeholder to deal with the situation.

The 'section 48' notice

Another important protection for leaseholders is found in section 48 of the Landlord and Tenant Act 1987. This was designed to deal with the situation in which freeholders seek to avoid their responsibilities by (to put it bluntly) doing a disappearing act. Sometimes freeholders would provide no address or telephone number or other means of contact, meaning that leaseholders were unable to hold the freeholder to his side of the agreement. Sections 47 and 48 therefore lay down that the freeholder must formally notify the leaseholder of his name and give an address within England and Wales at which he can be contacted, and that this information must be repeated on every demand for rent or service charge. This has proved especially valuable for leaseholders where the freeholder lives abroad, or is a company based abroad. It should be noted that the address does not have to be the freeholder's home, nor, if the freeholder is a company, its registered office; often it will be the address of a solicitor or property management company, or simply an accommodation address. But the key point is that any notice, or legal writ, is validly served if sent to that address, and the freeholder is not allowed to claim that it never came to his notice.

Good management

The freeholder is under an obligation to ensure that their management responsibilities are carried out in a proper and appropriate way. In particular fire safety responsibilities. Leaseholders can take the freeholder to court if they believe they can show that they are not receiving the standard of management to which they are entitled. This may be an expensive and lengthy process but it better than the alternative, sometimes resorted to by leaseholders, of withholding rent or service charge. This is risky because, whatever the shortcomings of the freeholder's management, it puts the leaseholders in breach of the conditions of their lease and, as such, demonstrably in the wrong (even if the freeholder may be in the wrong as well). It may be that leaseholders need more information so that they can decide whether the management is satisfactory. If so, there is power under the Leasehold Reform, Housing and Urban Development Act 1993 for a management audit to be demanded by an auditor acting on behalf of at least two-thirds of the qualifying leaseholders. Qualifying leaseholders are those with leases of residential property originally granted for 21 years or more and requiring them to contribute to the cost of services. The purpose of the audit, the costs of which must be met by the leaseholders demanding it, is to discover whether the freeholder's duties are being carried out efficiently and effectively. The auditor is appointed by the leaseholders and must be either a qualified accountant or a qualified surveyor and must not live in the block concerned. The auditor has the right to demand papers from the freeholder and can go to court if they are not produced.

In extreme cases a leaseholder can use the Landlord and Tenant Act 1987, section 24, to force the appointment of a managing agent to run the block instead of the freeholder. The leaseholder must serve a notice telling the freeholder what the problems are and warning that unless they are put right a First Tier Tribunal will be asked to appoint a managing agent. The FTT may make such an order if it satisfied that it is 'just and convenient'; the Act mentions, as specific examples where this may apply, cases where the freeholder is in breach of obligations under the lease and cases where service charges are being levied in respect of work of a poor standard or an unnecessarily high standard.

It should be noted that this procedure, although in some ways it resembles the procedures for collective enfranchisement in Chapter Four, differs from them in that it can be carried out by any individual leaseholder; it does not require the consent of a majority. Note too that the procedure is not available if the freeholder is a local authority, a registered housing association, or the Crown.

A Recognised Tenants' Association (RTA), where there is one, has additional rights to be consulted about managing agents. The RTA can serve a notice requiring the freeholder to supply details of the managing agent and the terms of the management agreement. Recognised Tenants' Associations are more important, however, in connection with service charges, explained in the Chapter Three. Leaseholders that are receiving a consistently poor or overpriced service may also wish to consider getting rid of the freeholder altogether by collective enfranchisement under the Leasehold Reform, Housing and Urban Development Act 1993 (see Chapter

Four). In addition, there is now the right to manage without proving fault, which is contained in the Commonhold and Leasehold Reform Act 2002. This right to manage entitles leaseholders to take over management of a building without having to prove any fault on the part of a landlord or pay any compensation.

Assignment of Leases

One of the most important characteristics of a lease - in marked contrast to most tenancies - is that it may be bought and sold. Usually, the freeholder has no say in this: the leaseholder may sell to whom he likes for the best price he can get, provided that the purchaser agrees to be bound by the terms of the lease. It is, however, usual for the lease to lay down that the freeholder must be informed of any change of leaseholder.

What actually happens when a lease is sold is that the vendor agrees to transfer to the buyer his rights and obligations under the lease. This is called 'Assignment' of the lease. In some types of housing the freeholder has the right to intervene if an assignment is envisaged. The housing may, for instance, be reserved for a particular category of resident, such as the retired, so the freeholder is allowed to refuse consent to the assignment if the purchaser does not qualify.

If the Lease Is Breached

If the terms of a lease are broken, the party offended against can go to a first-tier tribunal. This may be the leaseholder, for instance if the freeholder has failed to carry out a repair. But it is normally the freeholder that takes the leaseholder to court, for failure to pay ground rent or service charges or for breach of some other requirement.

It is for the tribunal, if satisfied that the lease has been breached, to decide what to do. The normal remedy will be that the offending party must pay compensation and that the breach (if it is still continuing) must be put right. It is also likely that the loser will be obliged to pay the winner's legal costs as well as his own, a penalty often considerably more severe than the requirement to pay compensation.

A much more severe remedy open to the freeholder if the leaseholder is in breach is forfeiture of the lease. This means what it says: the lease is forfeited to the freeholder. Forfeiture is sometimes threatened by the more aggressive class of freeholder but the good news for leaseholders is that in practice courts have shown themselves loathe to grant it except in very serious cases.

Since the Housing Act 1996 took effect, as amended by the 2002 Commonhold and Leasehold Reform Act, forfeiture for unpaid service charges has been made more difficult for freeholders. Where forfeiture is threatened for any reason other than failure to pay rent (which means the basic rent, not the service charge element), the freeholder must first serve a 'section 146 notice', so called after the relevant provision of the Law of Property Act 1925. In this he must state the nature of the breach of the lease, what action is required to put it right; if he wants monetary compensation for the breach, the notice must state this too. If the notice is not complied with, the freeholder may proceed to forfeit; but the leaseholder may go to court for relief from forfeiture.

The breach of the lease specified in the section 146 notice must have occurred during the twelve years preceding the notice. For breaches older than this, no valid section 146 notice can be served and so forfeiture is not available. If the freeholder breaches the lease, the leaseholder can go to court (usually a First Tier Tribunal) and seek an order requiring the freeholder to remedy the breach, to pay damages, or to do both.

The commonest type of breach complained of by leaseholders is failure to carry out repairs, and this explains why action by leaseholders is less usual; they know that if they force the freeholder to do repairs the costs will be recovered through service charges.

Legal action may be the best course if the dispute affects a single leaseholder: but if a number of leaseholders are involved they may well prefer to get rid of the freeholder altogether by collectively enfranchising their leases as described in Chapter Four.

****

SECTION 4

MANAGING SERVICE CHARGES

Ch. 4

Service Charges and the Law

By far the commonest cause of dispute between leaseholders and freeholders is the provision of services and the levying of service charges. In extreme cases, leaseholders have been asked to contribute thousands of pounds towards the cost of major repairs and have even suffered forfeiture of the lease if they are unable, or unwilling, to comply. Happily, such instances are rare; but even where the service charges are more moderate, they are often resented by leaseholders.

As was pointed out in chapter 1, there are now further charges to be levied by the landlord in connection with building safety and fire safety. This is achieved by an amendment to the Landlord and Tenant Act 1985, the insertion of a new section 17A to 17X. Although these are separate to service charges as we know them the charging regime will follow, more or less, the regime for service charges. Having covered the new building safety charges in chapter one, In this chapter I will deal with traditional service charge management.

The landlord of rented property is expected to meet

virtually all costs from the rent, whereas the freeholder of leasehold property has no rent to fall back on (apart from the normally negligible ground rent). How, then, are major costs to be met when they arise? The answer, of course, is from the service charge, which is, therefore, of central importance to the management of leasehold property.

From the freeholder's point of view, the logic of service charges is clear. It is perfectly reasonable for freeholders to point out:

- that leaseholders benefit from the work because it has maintained or improved their homes; and
- that the fact that the work has been done means that leaseholders will get a better price when they come to sell; and
- that people that own their homes freehold must find the money to meet costs of this kind.

In short, the purchase of a lease means the acceptance of a commitment to pay the appropriate share of costs. But this does not mean that leaseholders have no scope to challenge or query service charges. Under sections 18 to 30 of the Landlord and Tenant Act 1985, as amended by the 2002 Commonhold and Leasehold Reform Act, they have extensive legal protection against improper or unreasonable charging by freeholders, and this is discussed later in the Chapter. First, however, we should look at how a typical service charge is made up.

What goes into a Service Charge?

The lease will say how often service charges are levied: typically, monthly, six-monthly or annually. It is usual to collect the ground rent at the same time, but this is usually a small component of the bill. The service charge proper will normally consist of three elements:

- **The management fee** is the charge made by the freeholder, or the freeholder's agent, to cover the administrative cost of providing the service and collecting the charge. Usually, it will be much the same amount from one year to the next, but if major works have occurred the management fee will usually be higher to cover the extra costs of appointing and supervising contractors; 15% of the cost of the works is a common figure.

- **Direct costs (routine expenditure)** cover costs such as the supply of electricity to communal areas, building insurance, and the like. Again, these costs are likely to be fairly constant from year to year, so leaseholders know in advance roughly how much they are likely to have to pay.

- **Direct costs (exceptional expenditure)** cover costs that are likely to be irregular but heavy. They usually result from maintenance and repair, and it is because this component of the service charge is so unpredictable that it gives rise to so many problems. Where a house has been divided into leasehold flats, the freeholder's costs will usually be like what a normal homeowner would be obliged to pay; in other words, the costs may well be in the thousands (for a new roof, say) but are unlikely to be higher. Even so, a charge of £5000 for a new roof, even if divided between three or four flats, is still a major cost from the point of view of the individual leaseholder, especially if it is unexpected. The situation can be far worse in blocks of flats, where the costs of essential repair and maintenance may run into millions. Replacement of worn-out lifts, for example, is notoriously costly; and costs arising from structural defects are likely to be higher still.

Unreasonable Service Charges

General Principles

Sections 18 to 30 of the Landlord and Tenant Act 1985, as amended by the Landlord and Tenant Act 1987, and the Commonhold and Leasehold Reform Act 2002, grant substantial protection to leaseholders of residential property.

This protection was introduced after complaints of exploitation by unscrupulous leaseholders, who were alleged to be carrying out unnecessary, or even fictitious, repairs at extravagant prices, whilst not providing the information that would have enabled leaseholders to query the bill. The effect of the Acts is to require freeholders to provide leaseholders with full information about service charges and to consult them before expensive works are carried out.

A few leases, namely those granted under the right to buy by local authorities or registered housing associations, have some additional protection under the Housing Act 1985 (see below), but sections 18 to 30 apply to all residential leases where the service charge depends on how much the freeholder spends. They set out the key rules that freeholders must observe in order to recover the cost, including overheads, of 'services, repairs, maintenance or insurance', as well as the freeholder's costs of management. It should be noted that failure by leaseholders to pay the service charge does not relieve the freeholder of the obligation to provide the services.

The freeholder's remedy is to sue the leaseholder for the outstanding charges, or even to seek forfeiture of the lease (see below). Section 19 of the Landlord and Tenant Act 1985, as amended, provides the key protection to leaseholders by laying down that service charges are recoverable only if they

are 'reasonably incurred' and if the services or works are of a reasonable standard. This means that the charge:
- must relate to some form of 'service, repair, maintenance, or insurance' that the freeholder is required to provide under the lease;
- must be reasonable (that is, the landlord may not recover costs incurred unnecessarily or extravagantly);
- may cover overheads and management costs only if these too are reasonable.

In addition, the charge must normally be passed on to the leaseholders within 18 months of being incurred, and in some cases the freeholder must consult leaseholders before spending the money. These points are covered below.

The Housing Act 1996 (amended by the Commonhold and Leasehold Reform Act 2002) gave leaseholders new powers to refer service charges to the Leasehold Valuation Tribunal (LVT). LVT's have been replaced by First Tier Tribunals (introduced in July 2013)

The First Tier tribunal
Leaseholders can apply to the First-tier Tribunal (Property Chamber) to deal with disputes about service charges, repairs, extending leases or buying the freehold.

What disputes the tribunal deals with

If you own a leasehold flat or house and can't resolve a dispute with your freeholder, you may be able to apply to a tribunal for a decision. This tribunal can help with disputes over leasehold problems, such as:

- insuring the building
- the amount billed for service charges
- the quality of services such as cleaning and maintenance
- extending your lease
- buying the freehold

How to apply to the tribunal

The tribunal that deals with leaseholder disputes is called the First-tier Tribunal (Property Chamber). There are five regional tribunals. You can find details of your local tribunal from HM Courts & Tribunals Service. Apply to the tribunal using the correct form. This is available from Gov.uk. Send the form to the regional tribunal that covers your area. The address is on the form. The tribunal contacts you to tell you if it can consider your case. You may be asked to provide more information. You can ask for a hearing or the case can be decided on the evidence you and the freeholder send. Find out more from Gov.uk about what happens at a tribunal hearing.

Costs of taking a case to the tribunal

You may have to pay a fee (currently £100 at 2024) to apply to the tribunal. You can apply for an exemption or a reduced fee if you receive certain benefits or have a low income. If the problem affects more than one leaseholder, you can apply together and share the costs. You may have to pay a surveyor, property manager or a solicitor. In limited cases the tribunal can order the freeholder to compensate you. If you win the case, the tribunal may be able to order the freeholder to refund your application fee. Some freeholders can include their legal costs in your service charge bill.

The tribunal's decision

The tribunal's decision is binding on you and the freeholder. You might need to take court action to recover any money your freeholder owes you.

What the tribunal can decide-Disputes about service charges

The tribunal can consider if a service charge is payable, and if so how much you must pay.

Disputes about repairs

The tribunal can change what your lease says about maintenance and repairs if what's said is unclear or doesn't cover the issue in dispute.

Disputes about poor management

The tribunal can appoint a new manager if you can prove your building is being badly managed. The freeholder would still own the property but would lose the right to manage it.

Lease extension disputes

The tribunal can set a price for extending your lease or buying the freehold if you and the freeholder haven't been able to agree.

Appeals against the tribunal's decision

You may be able to appeal against the tribunal's decision. You can usually only do this if the tribunal has acted unfairly or didn't follow the correct procedures. You can't appeal because you don't like the tribunal's decision.

Service Charge demands

Section 153 of the 2002 Commonhold and Leasehold Reform Act states that all demands for service charges must be accompanied by a summary of leaseholder's rights and obligations. Accordingly, a leaseholder can withhold payment of charges if such a summary is not contained with a demand. Where a tenant withholds charges under section 153, the sections of a lease pertaining to payment of charges will not apply for the period for which the charge is withheld.

Sample summary of rights and obligations

Service Charges - Summary of tenants' rights and obligations

1. This summary, which briefly sets out your rights and obligations in relation to variable service charges, must by law accompany a demand for service charges. Unless a summary is sent to you with a demand, you may withhold the service charge. The summary does not give a full interpretation of the law and if you are in any doubt about your rights and obligations you should seek independent advice.

2. Your lease sets out your obligations to pay service charges to your landlord in addition to your rent. Service charges are amounts payable for services, repairs, maintenance, improvements, insurance or the landlord's costs of management, to the extent that the costs have been reasonably incurred.

3. You have the right to ask a First Tier Tribunal to determine whether you are liable to pay service charges for services, repairs, maintenance, improvements, insurance or management. You may make a request before or after you have paid the service charge. If the tribunal determines that the service charge is payable, the tribunal may also determine-

- who should pay the service charge and who it should be paid to;
- the amount;
- the date it should be paid by; and
- how it should be paid.

However, you do not have these rights where-
- a matter has been agreed or admitted by you;
- a matter has already been, or is to be, referred to arbitration or has been determined by arbitration and you agreed to go to arbitration after the disagreement about the service charge or costs arose; or a matter has been decided by a court.

4. If your lease allows your landlord to recover costs incurred or that may be incurred in legal proceedings as service charges, you may ask the court or tribunal, before which those proceedings were brought, to rule that your landlord may not do so.

5. Where you seek a determination from a First Tier tribunal, you will have to pay an application fee and, where the matter proceeds to a hearing, a hearing fee, unless you qualify for a waiver or reduction. The total fees payable will not exceed £500, but making an application may incur additional costs, such as professional fees, which you may also have to pay.

6. A First Tier tribunal has the power to award costs against a party to any proceedings where-
   o it dismisses a matter because it is frivolous, vexatious or an abuse of process; or
   o it considers a party has acted frivolously, vexatiously, abusively, disruptively or unreasonably.
   o The Upper Tribunal (Lands Chamber) has similar powers when hearing an appeal against a decision of a First Tier Tribunal.
7. If your landlord-
   o proposes works on a building or any other premises that will cost you or any other tenant more than £250, or
   o proposes to enter into an agreement for works or services which will last for more than 12 months and will cost you or any other tenant more than £100 in any 12 month accounting period,

then your contribution will be limited to these amounts unless your landlord has properly consulted on the proposed works or agreement or a First Tier Tribunal has agreed that consultation is not required.

You have the right to apply to the First-Tier tribunal to ask it to determine whether your lease should be varied on the grounds that it does not make satisfactory provision in respect of the calculation of a service charge payable under the lease.

8. You have the right to write to your landlord to request a written summary of the costs which make up the service charges. The summary must-
   o cover the last 12 month period used for making up the accounts relating to the service charge ending no later than the date of your request, where the accounts are made up for 12 month periods; or
   o cover the 12 month period ending with the date of your request, where the accounts are not made up for 12 month periods.
   o The summary must be given to you within 1 month of your request or 6 months of the end of the period to which the summary relates, whichever is the later.
9. You have the right, within 6 months of receiving a written summary of costs, to require the landlord to provide you with reasonable facilities to inspect the accounts, receipts and other documents supporting the summary and for taking copies or extracts from them.
10. You have the right to ask an accountant or surveyor to carry out an audit of the financial management of the premises containing your dwelling, to establish the obligations of your landlord and the extent to which

the service charges you pay are being used efficiently. It will depend on your circumstances whether you can exercise this right alone or only with the support of others living in the premises. You are strongly advised to seek independent advice before exercising this right.

11. Your lease may give your landlord a right of re-entry or forfeiture where you have failed to pay charges which are properly due under the lease. However, to exercise this right, the landlord must meet all the legal requirements and obtain a court order.

12. A court order will only be granted if you have admitted you are liable to pay the amount or it is finally determined by a court, tribunal or by arbitration that the amount is due. The court has wide discretion in granting such an order and it will take into account all the circumstances of the case.

Consultation with Leaseholders

Section 20 of the LTA 1985, which is the area of the Act dealing with the landlords obligation to consult leaseholders over both major expenditure, and also long-term agreements for the provision of services, has been substituted by section 151 of the 2002 Commonhold and Leasehold Reform Act.

**

Major works and long-term agreements

Section 151 provides extra protection where the cost of works is more than £250 per leaseholder. Therefore, if a landlord owns a block of 20 flats and wishes to spend £8,000 on repairs, the limit above which he will have to legally consult is £5,000. Costs above this level are irrecoverable (except, sometimes, when the works are urgent) unless the freeholder has taken steps to inform and consult tenants. If the leaseholders are represented by a recognised tenants' association, i.e. formally constituted and recognised by the landlord as well as leaseholders, they must also receive copies of the consultation notices along with individual leaseholders.

In relation to long-term agreements, these are agreements over 12 months. Such agreements may be those for servicing lifts. They do not include contracts of employment. The consultation limit for long term contracts is now £100 per person per annum. If the amount exceeds this then consultation must be carried out. The steps in the consultation procedure are as follows:

Landlords statement of why works are necessary. There is a requirement for the landlord to state why he considers the works or the agreement to be necessary. This is defined by a 1-month period within which the landlord must take account of all responses from leaseholders. All letters and responses have to be prepared in accordance with the requirements of the Act (2002 CLRA).

Estimates. Following this initial stage, at least two estimates must be obtained, of which at least one must be from someone wholly unconnected with the freeholder (obviously a building firm that the freeholder owns or works for is not 'wholly unconnected'; nor is the freeholder's managing agent).

Notification to leaseholders. The freeholder must either display a copy of the estimates somewhere they are likely to be seen by everyone liable to pay the service charge, or (preferably) send copies to everyone liable to pay the service charge.

Consultation The notification must describe the works to be carried out and must seek comments and observations, giving a deadline for replies and an address in the UK to which they may be sent. The deadline must be at least a month after the notice was sent or displayed.

Freeholder's response. The freeholder must 'have regard' to any representations received. This does not mean, of course, that the freeholder must do what the leaseholders say. It does mean, however, that the freeholder must consider any comments received, and good freeholders often demonstrate that they have done so by sending a reasoned reply. Therefore, a consultation period will usually be a minimum of 60 days from notification to instructions to carry out works. If a service charge is challenged in court for failure to follow these procedures, it is a defence for the freeholder to show that the works were urgent. However, the court would need to be satisfied that the urgency was genuine and that the freeholder behaved reasonably in the circumstances.

Section 151 is important because it gives the leaseholders notification of any unusual items in the offing and gives them an opportunity to raise any concerns and objections. If the leaseholder has any reservations at all, it is vital that they be put before the freeholder at this stage. It is highly unlikely, in the event of legal action later, that the court will support a leaseholder who raised no objection until the bill arrived. It is common for freeholders and their agents to fail to comply with the requirements of section 151. This comment applies not only where the freehold is owned by an individual or a relatively small organisation (where mistakes might be more understandable) but also where the freeholder is a large, well-resourced body like a local authority. As a result, leaseholders are often paying service charges that are not due, so all leaseholders should, before paying a service charge containing unusual items, ensure that section 151, if it applies, has been scrupulously followed. If not, they can refuse to pay.

Other Protection for Leaseholders-**Grant-aided works:**

If the freeholder has received a grant towards the cost of

carrying out the works, the amount must be deducted from the service charge levied on leaseholders.

Late charging

Service charge bills may not normally include costs incurred more than eighteen months earlier. The freeholder may, however, notify leaseholders within the eighteen-month period that they will have to pay a certain cost, and then bill them later. This might happen if, for instance, the freeholder is in dispute with a contractor about the level of a bill or the standard of work.

Pre-charging

Sometimes a lease will contain a provision allowing the freeholder to make a charge to cover future costs besides those already incurred. This practice, which is perfectly lawful, may be in the interests of the leaseholders by spreading over a longer period the cost of major works. It is, however, subject to the same requirement of reasonableness.

Court costs

Section 20C of the LTA 1985, provides protection against a specific abuse of the service charge system by freeholders. Previously, freeholders tended to regard their legal costs as part of the process of managing the housing and thus as recoverable from leaseholders. Such an attitude is not necessarily unreasonable. For example, if the freeholder is suing a builder for poor work, he is, in effect, acting on behalf of all the leaseholders and it is fair that they should pay any legal costs.

Service charges held on trust

Section 42 of the Landlord and Tenant Act 1987 (as amended by the 2002 CLRA) further strengthened the position of leaseholders by laying down that the freeholder, or the freeholder's agent, must hold service charge monies in a suitable trust fund that will ensure that the money is protected and cannot be seized by the freeholder's creditors if the freeholder goes bankrupt or into liquidation.

However, public sector freeholders, notably local authorities and registered housing associations, are exempt from this requirement.

Insurance

Usually, the lease provides for the landlord to arrange the insurance of the building (not the contents) and charge the cost as a service charge. This is the normal arrangement for buildings divided into flats, since it is important that there should be one single policy covering all risks to the building as a whole. It is normally recovered as part of the service charges and therefore the cost of the insurance may be challenged before or verified by the LVT in the usual way.

Where a service charge consists of or includes an amount payable for insurance, an individual leaseholder or the secretary of a recognized tenants' association may ask the landlord for a written summary of the policy or an opportunity to inspect and take copies of the policy.

The request must be made in writing and the landlord must comply within 21 days of receiving it. Where the request is for a written summary, the summary must show:

– the sum for which the property is insured;
– the name of the insurer;
– the risks covered in the policy.

The landlord can only be required to provide the summary once in each insurance period (usually a year).

Where the request is for sight of the policy, the landlord must provide reasonable access for inspection of the policy and any other relevant documents which provide evidence of payment, including receipts, and facilities for copying them. Alternatively, the request may be for the landlord to provide the copies of the policy and specified documents himself and to send them to the leaseholder or association or arrange for them to be collected.

'Period of Grace'

When a dwelling is sold under the right to buy by a local authority or non-charitable housing association, the purchaser is given an estimate of service charges for the following five years. This estimate is the maximum recoverable during that time. Some purchasers under the right to buy have, however, had a very rude shock when the five-year period of grace expires - see *Exceptionally High Service Charges* below.

The role of a recognised tenants' association

The tenants who are liable to pay for the provision of services may, if they wish, form a recognised tenants' association (RTA) under section 29 of the Landlord and Tenant Act 1985. Note that leaseholders count as tenants for this purpose (see Chapter One, where it explained that legally the two terms are interchangeable). If the freeholder refuses to give a notice recognising the RTA, it may apply for recognition to any member of the local Rent Assessment Committee panel. An important benefit of having a RTA is that it has the right, at the beginning of the consultation process, to recommend persons or organisations that should be invited to submit estimates. However, the freeholder is under no obligation to accept these recommendations.

Another advantage is that the RTA can, whether the freeholder likes it or not, appoint a qualified surveyor to advise on matters relating to service charges. The surveyor has extensive rights to inspect the freeholder's documentation and take copies and can enforce these rights in court if necessary.

Statement of accounts to leaseholders

Under section 152 of the Commonhold and Leasehold Reform Act 2002, which has substituted s.21 of the Landlord and Tenant Act 1985, a landlord must supply a statement of accounts to each tenant by who service charges are payable, in relation to each accounting period.

These accounts deal with:

a) Service charges of the tenant and the tenants of dwellings associated with his dwelling
b) Relevant costs relating to those service charges
c) The aggregate amount standing to the credit of the tenant and the tenants of those dwellings at the beginning and the end of the accounting period in question.

This statement of account must be supplied to the tenant not later than six months after the accounting period. A certificate of a qualified auditor must be supplied and, in addition, a summary of the rights and obligations of the tenant in relation to service charges must be supplied.

Challenging Service Charges

The Landlord and Tenant Act not only allows leaseholders to act against unreasonable behaviour by the freeholder; it also enables them to take the initiative. This is done in two ways: by giving leaseholders rights to demand information, and by allowing them to challenge the reasonableness of the charge.

Right to require information

Leaseholders have the right to ask freeholders for a written summary of costs counting towards the service charge. This is contained within s.22 of the Landlord and Tenant Act 1985, as amended by s.154 of the Commonhold and Leasehold Reform Act 2002. Such a summary must cover either the twelve months up to the point where it was requested or, if accounts are drawn up annually, the last complete twelve-month accounting period before the request was made. It must be sent to the leaseholder within 21 days of the request or within six months of the end of the period it covers, whichever is the later.

Failure to provide it without reasonable excuse is a criminal offence carrying a maximum fine of £2500.

The law lays down some minimum requirements for the summary. It must:
- o cover all the costs incurred during the twelve months it covers, even if they were included in service charge

bills of an earlier or later period (see above for late charging and pre-charging);

- o show how the costs incurred by the freeholder are reflected in the service charges paid, or to be paid, by leaseholders;
- o say whether it includes any work covered by a grant (see above);
- o distinguish: (a) those costs incurred for which the freeholder was not billed during the period; (b) those for which he was billed and did not pay; (c) those for which he paid bills.

If it covers five or more dwellings, the summary must, in addition, be certified by a qualified accountant as being a fair summary, complying with the Act, and supported by appropriate documentation. The purpose of section 22, as amended, is to put leaseholders in a position to challenge their service charges. After receiving the summary, the leaseholder has six months in which to ask the freeholder to make facilities available so that he can inspect the documents supporting the summary (bills, receipts, and so on) and take copies or extracts. The freeholder must respond within a month and make the facilities available within the two months following that; the inspection itself must be free, although the freeholder can make a reasonable charge for the copies and extracts. Failure to provide these facilities, like failure to supply the summary, is punishable by a fine of up to £2500.

Very similar rules apply where the lease allows, or requires, the freeholder to take out insurance against certain contingencies, such as major repair, and to recover the premiums through the service charge. This is not unreasonable and will, indeed, often be in the interests of leaseholders. The danger is, however, that the freeholder, knowing that the premiums are, in effect, being paid by someone else, has no incentive to shop around for the best deal. Section 30A of the Landlord and Tenant Act 1985 therefore lays down that leaseholders, or the secretary of the recognised tenants' association if there is one, may ask the freeholder for information about the policy. Failure to supply it, or to make facilities to inspect relevant documents available if requested to do so, is an offence incurring a fine of up to £2500.

Challenging the reasonableness of a service charge

Any leaseholder liable to pay a service charge, and for that matter any freeholder levying one, may refer the charge to a First Tier Tribunal to determine its reasonableness. This may be done at any time, even when the service in question is merely a proposal by the freeholder (for instance, for future major works). But the FTT will not consider a service charge if:

- it has already been approved by a court; or
- if the leaseholder has agreed to refer it to arbitration; or
- if the leaseholder has agreed it.

The first of these exceptions is obvious and the second is unlikely to apply very often. The third one is the problem: leaseholders should be careful, in their dealings with freeholders, to say or do nothing that could be taken to imply that they agree with any service charge that is in any way doubtful. The FTT will consider:

- whether the freeholder's costs of services, repairs, maintenance, insurance, or management are reasonably incurred;
- whether the services or works are of a reasonable standard; and
- whether any payment required in advance is reasonable.

The fees for application to a FTT can be obtained from the FTT and will usually change annually. Appeal against a FTT decision is not to the courts but to the Lands Tribunal. By section 19 of the Landlord and Tenant Act 1985, any service charge deemed unreasonable by the FTT is irrecoverable by the freeholder. The determination of service charges by the FTT also plays an important part in the rules governing the use of forfeiture to recover service charges. .

Forfeiture for Unpaid Service Charges

Forfeiture was mentioned at the end of Chapter Two. Briefly, it is the right of the freeholder to take possession of the property if the leaseholder breaches the lease. By section 81 of the Housing Act 1996, as amended by the 2002 Commonhold and Leasehold Reform Act, forfeiture for an unpaid service charge is available to the freeholder only if:

- the leaseholder has agreed the charge; or
- the charge has been upheld through arbitration or by a court or First Tier Tribunal.

Regarding the first of these, it is necessary only to reiterate the warning to leaseholders to say or do nothing that could possibly be construed as representing their agreement to any service charge about whose legitimacy they have the slightest doubt. Regarding the second, it should be noted that where the leaseholder has not agreed the service charge, court proceedings or formal arbitration are necessary before the freeholder can forfeit the lease.

Exceptionally High Service Charges

So far, this Chapter has focused on service charges of normal proportions that, however unforeseen and unwelcome they may be, should be within the means of the great majority of leaseholders. A minority of leaseholders, however, face the much more serious problem of consistently very high service charges. Where the cause is sharp practice by the freeholder, or failure to observe the legal requirements, the leaseholder can look for protection to the Landlord and Tenant Act as described above. Often, however, the freeholder is not to blame rather, the problem is that the work is genuinely necessary and unavoidably expensive. In this situation, and provided the landlord carefully follows the procedures laid down, the Landlord and Tenant Act offers no protection.

In what sort of housing is this most likely to occur? It is more likely to affect flats than houses because flats tend to contain potentially very expensive components such as lifts or communal arrangements for heating or ventilation. They are also more likely to have been built using construction methods or designs in vogue at one time but since found to lead to serious maintenance problems and high costs, whereas house building seems to be innately conservative and resistant to innovation: for instance, many blocks of flats contain asbestos, but very few houses. All these problems apply to flats in general, but there is an additional problem with blocks of flats owned by local authorities and housing associations: namely that, unlike blocks of flats developed by commercial owners for sale, they are likely to combine rented properties, let to periodic tenants in the usual way, with leasehold properties, sold at some point in the past under the right to buy or some similar scheme. These 'mixed managed' blocks present special problems for both categories of resident as well as the freeholder.

Clearly, there is no satisfactory way to resolve this problem. In a privately developed block, occupied wholly by leaseholders, the freeholder might possibly be prevailed upon to delay the repairs for a time if the leaseholders are prepared to put up with the poor conditions; but the Council can hardly be expected to take the same view when most of the residents are periodic tenants. Both the Council and the periodic tenants are likely to argue that the leaseholders are being asked to do no more than they agreed to do when they bought their leases.

All this book can do is warn prospective leaseholders of the serious problems that can arise in a minority of cases and suggest some of the questions that they should ask before signing the lease.

What is the condition of the building as a whole?

No one would buy a house, or an individual flat, without looking closely at its condition and estimating how much money it may need to have spent on it. But, when a flat is being bought, whether it is purpose-built or a conversion, it is equally important to look at the entire building of which it forms a part. The vendor should be asked for copies of past service charges, the freeholder should be asked whether major work is likely in the foreseeable future and what it is likely to cost, and an independent surveyor should be asked to report.

What is the leaseholder's liability?

The lease will specify what the leaseholder must pay for. Sometimes it will require him to contribute to things from which he does not benefit. For example, it is common for even ground floor leaseholders to be expected to contribute to the costs of the lifts; and some leaseholders, having paid out of their own pockets to replace their windows, are outraged to discover, when the freeholder has the windows of the whole block renewed, that they are required to pay a share of the cost. Provisions such as these are much resented by many leaseholders, who argue that they are unfair; but the time to object to such unfairness is before signing the lease, not many years later when the bills come in. It is therefore essential that anyone proposing to enter into a lease should first consult a solicitor.

Is there a 'period of grace' or other safeguard?

Right to buy leases contain an estimate of service charges for five years following the sale and that is the maximum that the Council may charge. Many purchasers, reassured by this, have signed the lease without paying much attention to the likely level of service charges thereafter, expecting perhaps to have sold at a profit and moved on before the five years expire. If so, they have been reminded of what many people forgot during the 1980s: that property prices can go down as well as up. In short, it is unwise to rely on a 'period of grace' to provide anything other than short-term relief; and in particular it is unwise to speculate on the future behaviour of the housing market.

Ground rent demands

Ground rents are charged by freeholders, to leaseholders and are usually fixed annual charges, and can vary greatly. Under section 166 of the Commonhold and Leasehold Reform Act 2002, it is the duty of all landlords to give formal notice of a demand for ground rents. A sample notice is set out below.

FORM OF RENT DEMAND NOTICE
COMMONHOLD AND LEASEHOLD REFORM ACT 2002,
SECTION 166

NOTICE TO LONG LEASEHOLDERS OF RENT DUE

To *(insert name(s) of leaseholder(s))*:

This notice is given in respect of *(address of premises to which the long lease relates)*

It requires you to pay rent of £............on *(insert date)* (note 2)................

This rent is payable in respect of the period *(state period)*

[In accordance with the terms of your lease the amount of £.... is/was due on *(insert date.............*

on which rent due in accordance with the lease).] (note 3)

Payment should be made to *(insert name of landlord(s) or if payment to be made to an agent, name of agent)* at *(insert address)*

This notice is given by *(insert name of landlord(s) and, if not given above, address)*

NOTES FOR LEASEHOLDERS

Read this notice carefully. It sets out the amount of rent due from you and the date by which you must pay it. You are advised to seek help immediately, if you cannot pay, or dispute the amount,. Those who can help you include a citizens' advice bureau, a housing advice centre, a law centre and a solicitor. Show this notice and a copy of your lease to whoever helps you. The landlord may be able to claim additional sums from you if you do not pay by the date specified in this notice. You have the right to challenge the reasonableness of any additional sums at a leasehold valuation tribunal.

Section 167 of the Commonhold and Leasehold Reform Act 2002 and regulations made under it prevent your landlord from forfeiting your lease for non-payment of rent, service charges or administration charges (or a combination of them) if the amount owed is £350 or less, or none of the unpaid amount has been outstanding for more than three years.

NOTES FOR LANDLORDS

I. If you send this notice by post, address it to the leaseholder at the dwelling in respect of which the payment is due, unless he has notified you in writing of a different address in England and Wales at which he wishes to be given notices under section 166 of the Commonhold and Leasehold Reform Act 2002.

2. This date must not be *either* less than 30 days or more than 60 days after the day on which this notice is given *or* before that on which the leaseholder would have been liable to make the payment in accordance with the lease.

3. Include this statement only if the date for payment is not the same as the date determined in accordance with the lease.

****

SECTION 5
PURCHASING THE FREEHOLD AND EXTENDING THE LEASE

Chapter 5

Purchasing the Freehold and Extension of Leases

The new provisions of the 2024 Leasehold and Freehold Reform Act 2024

The LFRA 2024 has introduced provisions which directly affect leaseholders and those seeking to purchase a freehold. The Act strengthens existing consumer rights for homeowners and introduces new ones. It introduces fundamental changes to the valuation methodology and legal process with a view to making it cheaper, easier, fairer, and more transparent for leaseholders to extend their leases and buy their freeholds.

The key provisions of the Act include:
- Longer lease terms. Leaseholders can now extend their leases by an additional 990 years with ground rent reduced to a nominal 'peppercorn' rent, removing the need for leaseholders to extend their leases more than once.

- The Act introduces a majority ban on leasehold houses, with only a very limited category of permitted leasehold houses allowed outlined in the Act.
- The abolition of marriage value will reduce the premium payable significantly for leases of less than 80 years. Marriage value is the increase in the value of the property following the completion of the lease extension, reflecting the additional market value of the longer lease.
- The Act also removes the two-year ownership requirement for extending leases or purchasing the freehold, allowing new leaseholders to act immediately.
- Mixed-use buildings may now qualify to buy their freeholds and the right to manage (RTM) increasing the commercial property element from 25% to 50% of floor area to allow a building to qualify for enfranchisement or RTM.

Freeholders will now be required to pay their own costs except in low-value claims and can now be forced to retain any non-participant flats or commercial leases in collective enfranchisement claims.

It should be noted that, at the time of writing the date for fully implementing the above provisions has yet to be determined. The law and procedure outlined reflects the current situation.

Enfranchising or extending leases

The sale of the freehold to leaseholders is called 'Enfranchisement'. Extending a lease means to extend it from its existing term, i.e. make longer.

The following are reasons for enfranchising or extending leases.

- a lease is a wasting asset and with every year that passes it gets shorter. Eventually, a flat will become unmortgagable and difficult to sell. Silly as it may sound, a lease with less than 80 years left to run is now regarded as being "short" and even leases with 80 to 85 years left may be difficult to sell
- a lease extension will preserve, and perhaps even increase, the value of a flat
- if leaseholders enfranchise, they can grant themselves extended leases
- many existing leases do not satisfy mortgage lenders' current requirements. If leaseholders enfranchise, they can rewrite leases to overcome that problem
- leaseholders may be unhappy with the management of their building.
- If they enfranchise, they can take control of the management

LEASEHOLD REFORM, HOUSING AND URBAN DEVELOPMENT ACT 1993

The area of leasehold enfranchisement has attracted a plethora of media and academic interest since its formal introduction in 1967 and has been amended and expanded over the past four decades. The right of long leaseholders to buy their landlord's interest outright or acquire an extended lease term, is unique to England and Wales and, perhaps unsurprisingly, has led to a number of legal challenges over the years. Landlords and tenants alike are anxious to protect their respective property interests in a market that shows no sign of abating. Consequently, this area of the law is continually evolving.

In general terms, the legislation confers two distinct rights: to purchase the freehold, either individually in relation to leasehold houses, or collectively for a block of flats, or to seek a lease extension.

Although these rights are curtailed by the statutory tests for qualification, changes to the legislation, introduced by the Commonhold and Leasehold Reform Act 2002, have made it easier than ever for leaseholders to make a claim. The requirement that leaseholders must have occupied the property in question for a period of two years (the so-called residence requirement) was largely swept away and replaced by a new, two-year ownership test. As mentioned above, The

2024 Leasehold and Freehold Reform Act has removed the two year ownership requirement for extending leases or purchasing the freehold, allowing **new** leaseholders to act immediately. The Act also removes the need for leaseholders to pay landlords costs when extending leases of purchasing a freehold.

The Collective Right to enfranchise-What is it?
This gives the right for tenants of flats acting together to purchase the freehold and any head leases of their building. In order for the building to qualify under the Act, it must:

- be an independent building or be a part of a building which is capable of independent development; and
- contain two or more flats held by qualifying tenants; and
- have at least two thirds of the flats held by qualifying tenants.

In order to be a qualifying tenant, you must have a long lease which means a lease which, when originally granted, was for a term of more than 21 years. However, you must not own three or more flats in the building. You cannot be a qualifying tenant if you hold a business lease. Notwithstanding the above, the building will not qualify if:

- it comprises four or less units and has a "resident freeholder";
- more than 25% of the internal floor space (excluding common parts) is used for non-residential purposes;
- the building is part of an operational railway.

How do I prepare for a claim?

Any qualifying tenant can give a notice to his landlord or the managing agent requiring details of the various legal interests in the block. This notice places no commitment on the tenant but the response to the notice should provide the tenant with the information necessary for him to ascertain whether the building contains a sufficient number of qualifying tenants for it to qualify.

Having established that the building qualifies, it is then advisable to ascertain whether you have a sufficient number of tenants who want to participate, both for the purpose of qualifying for enfranchisement and for the purpose of being able to finance the acquisition. In order to qualify for enfranchisement, you need to establish that the number of participating tenants comprises not less than one half of all the flats in the building. However, if there are only two flats in the building then both must participate.

When you have established that the building qualifies and that there is a sufficient number of qualifying tenants who wish to participate, then there are five further practical steps which should be taken before embarking on the enfranchisement procedure.

First, you need to establish what it is going to cost by obtaining a valuation. In simple terms, the price to be paid by the participating tenants to purchase the freehold of the building is the aggregate of:

- The building's investment value to the freeholder-the capitalised value of his ground rents and the value of his reversion (being the present freehold vacant possession value deferred for the unexpired term of the lease).
- One half of the marriage value-the increased value attributable to the freehold by virtue of the participating tenants being able to grant themselves extended leases at nil premium and a peppercorn rent. The marriage value attributable to a lease held by a participating tenant will be deemed to be nil if that lease has an unexpired term of more than 80 years at the date that the initial notice is given.
- Compensation for loss of value of other property owned by the freeholder, including development value consequent to the severance of the building from that other property.

The valuation date is the date that the claim notice is given. Value added to the flat of a participating tenant by tenant's improvements is disregarded in the valuation. For the purposes of calculating price, the tenants should take the advice of a properly qualified surveyor or valuer with experience in the field of enfranchisement and knowledge of the market.

In addition to the price and the participating tenants' own legal costs and valuation fees, the claimants will be required to reimburse the freeholder his legal costs and valuation fees.

Secondly, the participators will need to establish how to finance the cost of acquisition. It may, for example, be necessary for a number of participating tenants to seek a further advance from a Building Society or Bank. In particular, the participators will want to decide who is to finance the purchase of the non-participators' flats and on what basis.

Thirdly, it will be necessary to establish what vehicle the participating tenants should use in order to buy the freehold and how they will establish and regulate the relationship between themselves. In most cases, this is likely to be through a company structure, although in some circumstances a trust might be more appropriate. It should be noted that the participating tenants do not all have to have equal shares, so that the proportion of the shareholdings will be a matter for negotiation between them.

The 2002 Act provides for collective claims to be made through the mechanism of a Right to Enfranchise (RTE) company. However, those provisions have never been brought into force and it is unlikely that they will be.

Fourthly, the participating tenants should seek advice to establish whether there are tax implications to the transaction, both in relation to their individual positions and in relation to the vehicle chosen to buy the freehold.

Finally, the collective enfranchisement legislation provides no guidance or controls on the way in which the participating tenants should work together in order to acquire the freehold. Since the purchase may well involve substantial sums of money and is likely to take time to complete and, during this time, the participating tenants will be heavily reliant on each other for the performance of tasks within strict limits, it is strongly advised that, before embarking on a claim, the participating tenants should enter into a formal agreement (called a participation agreement) in order to regulate the relationship between them during the course of the claim.

How is the claim made?

It is important to be aware that most of the time limits imposed on the procedural stages of the claim are strict and a failure to do something within the required time frame can have dire consequences for the defaulter. It is therefore essential that, by the time you reach the next stage of the procedure, you are well organised and backed by expert professional advice.

The reason for this is that the next procedural step is the service by the participating tenants on the landlord of what the Act calls the initial notice – the notice which claims the right to collective enfranchisement. Costs start to run against the tenants from the time they serve the initial notice. Amongst other things this notice must specify:

- the extent of the property to be acquired – supported by a plan;
- full particulars of all the qualifying tenants in the building –not just the participating tenants;
- the price being offered for the freehold – the offer should be genuine;
- the name and address of the nominee purchaser – the person or company nominated by the participating tenants to conduct the negotiations and to buy the freehold on their behalf;
- the date by which the freeholder must give his counter-notice, being a date not less than two months from the date of the service of the initial notice.

The freeholder is likely to respond with a procedural notice requiring the participating tenants to deduce title. The freeholder's valuer is also likely to inspect the building for the purpose of carrying out a valuation.

Within the period specified in the initial notice, the freeholder must serve his counter-notice. First and foremost, this must state whether or not the claim is admitted. If it is not, then the participating tenants must decide if they wish to dispute the rejection through the courts. There are circumstances where the freeholder can resist a claim on the ground of redevelopment. If the claim is admitted, then the counter-notice must state, amongst other things:

- which of the proposals contained in the initial notice are acceptable;
- which of the proposals contained in the initial notice are not acceptable and what are the freeholder's counter-proposals –particularly on price;
- whether the freeholder wants a leaseback on any units in the building not held by a qualifying tenant (for example, a flat subject to a short term tenancy or a commercial unit).
- compensation for loss in value of other property owned by the freeholder, including development value consequent to sale

Disputes

If any terms of acquisition (including the price) remain in dispute after two months following the date of the counter-notice, then either party can apply to the First Tier tribunal for the matter in dispute to be determined. This application must be made within six months following the date of the counter-notice or the claim is lost. Most claims are settled by negotiation. If a tribunal is required to make a determination, then there is a right to appeal that decision to the Lands Tribunal if permission is given to do so.

Completion

Once the terms of acquisition have been agreed or determined by the First Tier Tribunal, then the matter reverts to a conveyancing transaction with the parties entering into a sale contract on the terms agreed or determined and thence to completion. If the matter proceeds to completion, then the participating tenants, through their nominee purchaser, will become the freeholder of the building, subject to the various flat leases. In effect, the participating tenants will replace the existing freeholder. This will put them in a position to grant themselves extended leases.

There may be taxation consequences on granting an extended lease, particularly for second homeowners. There will also be responsibilities. The participating tenants will become responsible for the management of the building and the administration of the service charge account in accordance with the covenants in the original leases.

If the nominee purchaser is a company, all participators will be shareholders, and some will be officers of that company. These are all matters on which clear professional advice will be needed. It is important to note that an individual tenant has no right to become a participating tenant – even if he is a qualifying tenant. It is a matter for the tenants to resolve between themselves. You can always ask to be allowed to join in, but you will have no remedy if refused. If a group does form without you – and does not need you – you may well find yourself left out.

However, if you are left out, that need not necessarily be the end of the road. This is because of the second major innovation that was introduced by the 1993 Act and subsequently amended by the 2002 CLARA – the individual right to acquire a new lease.

The individual right to extend leases-What is it?
The individual right to a statutory lease extension applies to all qualifying tenants of flats. The condition is that you must be the tenant of a flat which you hold on a long lease (i.e. a lease for an original term in excess of 21 years). Furthermore,

you must have owned the lease for at least two years before the date of the claim.

However, note the provisions of the 2024 Leasehold and Freehold Reform Act which state that new leaseholders are not bound by the two-year rule and can act immediately. The extension period is now 990 years for new leaseholders.

For the purpose of the lease extension, there is no limit to the number of flats you may own in the building, and you may extend any or all of them provided that the conditions are met. However, you cannot be a qualifying tenant if you hold a business lease. Prior to the 2002 Act, the personal representatives of a deceased tenant had no rights to make a claim, even where the deceased tenant was able to fulfill the qualifying conditions. However, such personal representatives can now make a claim provided that the right is exercised within a period of two years from the date of grant of probate.

What do I get?
If you qualify, then you will be entitled to acquire a new extended lease in substitution for your existing lease. This extended lease will be for a term expiring 90 years after the end of the current lease and will reserve a peppercorn rent throughout the term. Note the provisions for a 990 year lease

for new leaseholders under the 2024 Leasehold and Freehold Reform Act..

Broadly, the lease will otherwise be on the same terms as the existing lease but the landlord will have certain additional redevelopment rights, exercisable within 12 months before the expiration of the current lease term and within 5 years before the expiration of the extended lease.

The price

The price to be paid for the new lease will be the aggregate of:

- the diminution in value of the landlord's interest in the flat, consequent on the grant of the extended lease; being the capitalised value of the landlord's ground rent and the value of his reversion (being the present near-freehold vacant possession value deferred for the unexpired lease term);
- 50% of the marriage value (the additional value released by the tenant's ability to merge the extended lease with the existing lease) must be paid to the landlord although the marriage value will be deemed to be nil if the existing lease has an unexpired term of more than 80 years at the date of the claim;
- compensation for loss in value of other property owned by the freeholder, including development value, consequent on the grant of the new lease

The valuation date is the date of the claim notice. In addition to the price and the tenant's own legal costs and valuation fees, you will also be required to reimburse the freeholder his legal costs and valuation fees.

How do I claim?

The procedure to be followed is very similar to that for collective enfranchisement. It is therefore important to be aware that most of the time limits imposed on the procedural stages of the claim are strict and a failure to do something within the required time frame can have dire consequences for the defaulter.

The qualifying tenant can serve a preliminary notice to obtain information. Thereafter, he serves his notice of claim (in this case called the tenant's notice of claim) which amongst other things needs to state:

- a description of the flat – but not necessarily with a plan;
- sufficient particulars to establish that the lease qualifies;
- the premium being offered – it must be a bona fide offer;
- the terms of the new lease;

- the date by which the landlord must give the counter-notice, being a date not less than two months from the date of service of the tenant's notice.

The landlord is likely to respond with a procedural notice requiring payment of a deposit (equal to 10% of the premium being offered) and asking the tenant to deduce (prove) title. The landlord's valuer is also likely to inspect the flat for the purpose of carrying out a valuation.

Within the period specified in the tenant's notice, the landlord must serve his counter-notice. First and foremost, this must state whether or not the claim is admitted. If it is not, then the tenant must decide if he wishes to dispute the rejection through the courts.

However, unlike a collective enfranchisement claim where the nominee purchaser makes the application to the court in these circumstances, in the case of the statutory lease extension, it is the landlord who makes the application if he has refused the claim.

Enfranchisement - refusal

There are circumstances where the landlord can resist a claim on the ground of redevelopment. If the claim is admitted, then the counter-notice must state, amongst other things:

- which of the proposals contained in the tenant's notice are acceptable;
- which of the proposals contained in the tenant's notice are not acceptable and what are the landlord's counter-proposals – particularly the premium.

Disputes

If either the terms of the lease or the premium remain in dispute after two months following the date of the counter-notice, then either party can apply to the First Tier Tribunal for the matter in dispute to be determined.

This application must be made within six months following the date of the counter-notice or the claim is lost. Most claims are settled by negotiation. If a leasehold valuation tribunal is required to make a determination, then there is a right to appeal that decision to the Lands Tribunal if permission is given to do so

Completion

Once the terms of the lease and the premium have been agreed or determined by the First Tier Tribunal, then the matter reverts to a conveyancing transaction with the parties proceeding to completion of the new lease. The tenant can withdraw at any time and there are provisions for the tenant's notice to be considered withdrawn if certain strict time limits are not met by the tenant. As in collective enfranchisement, the tenant is at risk as to costs as from the date of his tenant's notice so it is essential to be prepared and to be properly advised before starting down the road to an extension.

A tenant's notice is capable of being assigned but only in conjunction with a contemporaneous assignment of the lease. It is common for a seller to serve a notice and then sell that notice with the lease to a purchaser, who will take over the claim. There is no limit to the number of times that a tenant can exercise this right – so long as he is prepared to pay the costs for doing so.

Enfranchisement of Houses

It is important to note that under the 2024 leasehold and Freehold Reform Act a majority ban on new leasehold houses has been introduced. Only a very limited number of houses will be permitted to be leasehold, as defined in the Act.

For current leaseholders of houses, The Leasehold Reform Act 1967, as amended by CLRA 2002, gives the tenant of a leasehold house who fulfils certain rules of qualification the right to acquire the freehold and any intermediate leases.

How do I qualify?

In looking at the rules of qualification under the 1967 Act, as amended there are three basic questions that need to be answered. First, does the building qualify. Secondly, does the lease qualify. Thirdly, does the tenant qualify. In order for the building to qualify, it must be a 'house'. This has developed a wide definition and can mean a shop with a flat above, or a building converted to flats. However, one essential feature is that there must be no material over or under-hang with an adjoining building (if there is, then it is likely to be a flat). The lease must comprise the whole of the house and it must be a long tenancy, i.e., a lease with an original term of more than 21 years. However, if it is a business tenancy, then it will not qualify if it is for an original term of 35 years or less.

The tenant must have owned the lease of the house for a period of at least two years before the date of the claim.

If a house is mixed use so that there is a business tenancy (for example a building comprising a shop with a flat above) or if the house includes a flat which is subject to a qualifying lease under the 1993 Act (see above), then the tenant is still required to fulfil a residence test. However, it is modified so that the tenant must occupy the house as his only or main residence only for two years or periods amounting in aggregate to two years in the preceding ten years. Prior to the 2002 Act, the personal representatives of a deceased tenant had no right to make a claim, even where the deceased tenant was able to fulfill the qualifying conditions. However, such personal representatives can now make a claim provided that the right is exercised within a period of two years from the date of grant of probate.

The Price

The 1967 act provides two distinct methods for valuing houses under the act. These are generally referred to by the relevant section of the 1967 act, as follows.

- Section 9 (1) – the house will be valued according to the original valuation basis, that is, the value of the site.
- Section 9 (1A), 9 (1C) – the house will be valued according to the special valuation basis, that is, the value of the house, including a share of the marriage value.

You and the landlord cannot choose which valuation to use. It depends on the qualification criteria.

Put simply:
- if the lease meets the original low-rent test and the house meets the value limits, the house will be valued according to the original valuation basis under section 9 (1) of the 1967 act; or

- in all other cases, including cases where the original lease had been extended under section 14 of the 1967 act, the house will be valued according to the special valuation basis.

Generally, if a house is valued using the special valuation basis of assessment, the price is much higher than it would be under the original valuation basis, so it is very important to work out which valuation method should be used.

By law, under both sets of rules, the freehold must be valued as if it were being sold on the open market by a willing seller to a willing buyer. The principles of the 1967 act are not to provide a forced bargain for the leaseholder, but to adequately compensate the landlord for the loss of their property by making sure the leaseholder pays a fair price, based as closely as possible on open-market values. It is difficult to assess an open-market value in the artificial situation created by the need to protect the leaseholder's rights. If you and the landlord cannot settle the price by negotiation, either of you can ask a First-tier Tribunal (Property Chamber) to settle the matter. The tribunal's role is not to decide in favour of either your or the landlord's valuation, but to make an independent decision. So, the tribunal's decision may not necessarily reflect either of the prices you or the landlord proposed.

As the leaseholder, you start the process of enfranchisement by serving a formal notice of claim to tell the landlord that you plan to use your right to buy the freehold. Once you have served this notice, you will be liable to pay the landlord's reasonable costs in dealing with it, so you should find out what these costs are likely to be before you begin the process. A valuation surveyor experienced in the law and with a good knowledge of the local property market will be able to help you.

You will need professional advice to confirm your rights and which valuation method should be use

How do I claim?

The procedure for a claim is relatively straightforward. The tenant serves his notice of claim, which is in prescribed form and needs to state (inter alia):

- a description of the house – but not necessarily with a plan;
- particulars to establish that the lease and tenant qualify;
- what the tenant thinks is the basis of valuation.

In addition to the price and the tenant's own legal costs and valuation fees, he will be required to reimburse the freeholder his legal costs and valuations fees.

The landlord is likely to respond with a procedural notice requiring payment of a deposit (equal to three times the rent payable under the lease) and asking the tenant to deduce title and (if a residence test is relevant) to produce evidence by statutory declaration that he fulfils the residence condition.

The landlord's valuer is also likely to inspect the house for the purpose of carrying out a valuation. The Act requires the landlord to state, within two months of the notice of claim being served, whether or not he admits the claim. If the claim is not admitted then the tenant must decide if he wishes to dispute the rejection through the courts. A freeholder cannot resist a claim on redevelopment grounds.

Disputes

If the claim is admitted and either the terms of the conveyance or the price remain in dispute after two months following the date of the notice of claim, then either party can apply to the First Tier Tribunal for the matter in dispute to be determined. There are no time limits on the making of this application.

Completion

Once the terms of the conveyance and the purchase price have been agreed or determined by the leasehold valuation tribunal, the matter reverts to a conveyancing transaction with the parties proceeding to completion.

The tenant can withdraw at any time up to one month following the determination of the purchase price. Unlike collective enfranchisement and statutory lease extension claims, there are no strict procedural time limits. However, the tenant is liable for the landlord's costs as from the date of his notice of claim.

Landlord and Tenant Act 1987: First Refusal

The Landlord and Tenant Act 1987 was chiefly concerned with enabling leaseholders to protect themselves against unreasonable service charges, and it made numerous amendments to tighten the rules originally laid down in the Landlord and Tenant Act 1985. In addition, it granted leaseholders the important right of first refusal if the freehold of their property is sold. It also allowed leaseholders to acquire the freehold if the property is being mismanaged: however, this right is little used because of the difficult procedures involved, and although it remains on the statute book it is likely to fall into complete disuse because the 2002 Act has now given leaseholders the same right without having to prove mismanagement.

The Right of First Refusal (RFR) is provided by Part 1 of the Landlord and Tenant Act 1987 (the 1987 Act) as amended by the Housing Act 1996.

Where a landlord is proposing to sell his interest in a building containing flats in relation to which the RFR exists, he must, by law, first offer it to the tenants before offering it on the open market. He must serve formal notices on the tenants telling them what he is intending and must provide time for them to consider the offer; he cannot sell to another party during that time, nor offer the interest to anyone else at a price less than that proposed to the tenants or on different terms. Breach of these legal obligations by the landlord is a criminal offence. If the landlord sells without providing the Right of First Refusal, the tenants can serve a notice on the new owner demanding details of the transaction, including the price paid; they can then take action to force the new owner to sell to them at the price he paid.

It is important to understand certain key principles of the RFR:

- it is not a means of forcing a landlord to sell his freehold interest in a property (this is provided by the enfranchisement provisions of the Leasehold Reform, Housing and Urban Development Act 1993). It is an opportunity for the tenants to purchase that interest before it is offered on the open market or by auction.
- the right follows a landlord's decision to sell and the tenants can only react to the landlord's offer. He can

withdraw the offer at any time before the contract is binding.
- the right is available both to leaseholders and regulated (fair rent) tenants but not to houses occupied as single dwellings.
- the price is set by the landlord, or by auction where the landlord decides to sell that way. There is no right for that price to be determined by a Leasehold Tribunal or anyone else. However, the landlord cannot sell or offer the interest to another party on different terms or at a lower price than that originally offered within 12 months of his notice, unless he again offers the Right to the existing tenants on the new terms and/or at the lower figure.
- the price set may, in some circumstances, be lower than that which could be achieved through a collective enfranchisement. However, it could also be higher.
- the requirement to make the offer and the procedure involved is set out in the Act. If a landlord fails to comply with any of these statutory requirements he commits a criminal offence. The requirements also apply where the landlord's interest is being sold by a Receiver, a Trustee in or an Executor following grant of probate. The right is not available to tenants of local

authorities, housing associations, nor, in some cases, where the landlord lives in the building.

Buildings, landlords and qualifying tenants

For the RFR to exist, the building, the landlord and the tenants must meet certain requirements.

The building

There are three requirements for the building to be subject to the RFR:

- it must contain at least two flats; and
- No more than 50% of the building to be in non-residential use; and
- more than 50% of the flats in the building must be held by 'qualifying tenants'.

The legislation does not define what is intended as a building, but it is generally understood to mean a separate building or, in some cases, a part of a building which may be divided vertically from another part. In the absence of a legal definition, a common sense approach should apply as to what normally constitutes a building and whether it is capable of development without substantially affecting the rest of the building. So, floors of flats above a shop are not a separate building but one half of a pair of semi-detached houses converted into flats is a separate building from its neighbour.

There must be at least two flats in the building, so the right does not apply to houses occupied as one unit - but will, of course, apply to a house which has been converted into flats. The building will be excluded from the RFR if more than 50% (excluding the common areas) is not in residential use, say offices or shops. The measurement excludes any common parts of the residential building, such as staircases, landings etc. The Act refers to parts of the premises occupied or intended to be occupied for non-residential purposes. A building could be excluded if it contained empty spaces which made up more than half the building which the landlord intended to use for non-residential purposes, such as storage.

The landlord

The RFR does not apply to the following landlords:
- most housing authorities (local Councils, New Towns and Development Corporations) also registered social landlords and fully mutual housing associations which are not registered;
- charitable housing trusts; and resident landlords who live in the building where the following two conditions apply:
- the building is not a purpose-built block of flats, that is, it must be a property, a house for example, which has

been converted into flats since its original construction; and
- the landlord genuinely lives in the building as his only or principal residence and has done so for more than 12 months.

Immediate landlord

The RFR only applies when the immediate landlord of the tenants decides to sell. The immediate landlord is the one to whom the rent or ground rent is paid and who will be entitled to vacant possession of the flat when the lease expires. Where a landlord has a lease for less than seven years (or longer, but which is terminable within the first seven years) his landlord is also subject to the RFR in relation to those premises.

Qualifying tenants-**The RFR is restricted to qualifying tenants.**

These include leaseholders and most fixed or periodic tenancies, but specifically excludes shorthold or assured tenancies, business and agricultural tenancies, tenancies which are dependant upon employment (and any sub-tenants of any of these). Someone who is a tenant of three or more flats in the building (as leaseholder or tenant) will not be a qualifying tenant of any of the flats and will not be entitled to the Right of First Refusal. The Procedure under the 1987 Act for the right of first refusal is as follows.

- The freeholder notifies all qualifying tenants of his desire to sell and of the price at which he is willing to do so (including any non-monetary element). The notice must state the proposed method of sale: for instance, by conveyance or by auction.
- The freeholder must give the qualifying tenants at least two months to respond; and, if they say they wish to buy, at least a further two months (28 days if the sale is to be by auction) to come up with a nominee purchaser to acquire the freehold on their behalf. This could conceivably be in an individual or an organisation that already exists but is much more likely to be a company set up specially for the purpose by the qualifying tenants, and under their control.
- During this period, the landlord and the qualifying tenants may wish to take the opportunity to negotiate the price.
- If a majority of the qualifying tenants have put forward a nominee purchaser and agreed with the freeholder on a price, the freeholder may not sell to anyone else.
- If the qualifying tenants fail to put forward a nominee purchaser, or if a mutually acceptable price is not agreed, the freeholder has twelve months to sell to someone else in accordance with the original notice (by auction, if that was the method specified; and in any other case for a price not less than that originally offered to the qualifying tenants).

If no sale has taken place within twelve months, the freeholder must start the procedure again from scratch if he wishes to sell.

****

SECTION 6

FORMING AND MANAGING A FLAT MANAGEMENT COMPANY

Chapter 6

The Formation of a Flat Management Company

Flat owners, although individuals in their own right, are joined in the need to ensure that the management of their flats and common areas is carried out cost effectively and efficiently. So far, in this book we have concentrated on the rights and obligations of leaseholders and freeholders. However, if leaseholders wish to exercise the right to enfranchise, as described in the previous chapter, or to simply purchase the freehold on offer from the landlord, then a vehicle for the ownership of the freehold and the management of the flats, will need to be created.

Each flat owner will want to ensure that a proper structure is in place for management and for enforcing obligations between flat owners and for how the building as a whole is maintained and ensured. To this end, many groups managing their flats through a flat management company will instruct a managing agent.

What is the purpose of a company set up to manage flats?

At the beginning of the book, the nature of a lease was outlined. Under the terms of flat leases, the flat owner will have entered into covenants which are inserted in the lease and are necessary for the efficient running of the block. Without some separate body enforcing the covenants, management of the building would break down. The block would soon fall into disrepair, the common areas remain unclean and untended and the overall appearance of the block would diminish, along with the value of the properties.

Although there are a number of ways of managing a block of flats, or a house split into flats, such as an individual ownership of the freehold, it is the flat management company which is the recommended vehicle for management of the freehold, after enfranchisement or a straight purchase of the freehold.

For the rest of this chapter we will discuss the setting up of such a company and how to go about administering it.

The management company

The company set up to own the freehold and to manage the leases and provide services will be a limited liability company. A limited company is a distinct entity having a separate legal capacity from its shareholders, or members. The company's members have control of the company that they exercise through voting rights. The company may be limited by shares or by guarantee. A limited company is defined by the concept of limited liability that means that the liability of the members to contribute to the debts of the company is limited. They will have either purchased shares in the company or guaranteed to contribute a fixed sum to the company.

In many cases, a proportion of flat owners in a block will not be interested in participating as members of a company, even though they own a share. Ultimate success of a flat management company will, usually, depend on the will and drive of a few members. Without this drive then the company will not come into being and effective management will not be delivered. If enough members are enthusiastic then a committee will need to be formed with delegated powers to be able to go forward and set up the limited company. A solicitor will need to be appointed to incorporate the company and to transfer ownership of the freehold from the freeholder to the management company. There will be a number of supporting requirements for the company such as:

- Banking facilities- the committee will need to arrange for a current account to be set up with a local bank, agree signatories to the account and provide the signed mandate for the bank. The bank will offer you further advice;

- Accountants will need to be appointed. This will certainly be the case where there is a lot of money flowing through the company and VAT is involved. If the cash flow is minimal then it may be the case that simple accounts are kept by the members of the committee, by someone with the requisite skills. However, this is a function that will need to be decided as soon as possible.
- The registered office will need to be decided upon.

Other areas of administration may be printed letterheads. Again, some thought should be given as to whether this is really necessary.

A company will have Memoranda and Articles of association. The memoranda and articles of association regulate the activities of the company and define what it can and cannot do. Flat management companies will usually have specific provisions in the articles, limiting membership of the company to those who own a flat in the block or house. Forms of articles used by flat management companies are normally created by the solicitors appointed to set up the company. Although there are model articles on companies house website these are not generally applicable to flat management companies.

Transferring ownership of the freehold to the new company

The solicitor acting on behalf of the flat owners in the conveyance of the freehold will have a duty to determine good title to the building. All aspects of the ownership of the building and any future matters that may affect ownership will be checked. Many of the tasks undertaken by a solicitor will be the same as if a property was being purchased in the normal way. Local authority searches will be undertaken and questions asked relating to any outstanding debts. The lease will be examined, with a particular emphasis on the provisions for payment of service charges and ground rent, when and how these should be paid and the financial year relating to the company. Of importance here is the question of conveyance of the freehold whilst there are outstanding arrears. Does the newly formed management company wish to undertake responsibility for outstanding arrears or will it insist that these are paid up before transfer? This is an important point and it is good practice to ensure that all arrears are paid up so that the company and its members are starting from a clean slate.

Appointment of officers

It is more than likely that all flat owners will be shareholders of the management company. As with all companies, shareholders will delegate the running of the company to appointed officers. This is necessary as otherwise the whole operation can lose focus and also disagreements can set in. Companies have a minimum legal requirement on formation- there must be at least two officers at formation, a Director and a Company secretary. There need only be one director in office at any one time.

The role of the company secretary is of particular importance as this person has the most work to do in administering the company, giving notice to the members of meetings, preparing notices, drafting resolutions, preparing minutes and filing all statutory forms. The latter task is important because failure to file accounts and annual returns to companies house results in an automatic fine, currently one hundred pounds.

The full details of company's house, the address and supporting information will be given on incorporation of the company. Most flat management companies, following incorporation, are best managed by a small committee of flat owners, with officers appointed to carry out specific tasks. This committee can rotate on a periodic basis, if needs be.

Common administrative requirements of a flat management company are as follows:
- Insurance
- Maintenance and repairs

- Banking
- Rent and service charge collection
- Preparation of annual budget estimates
- Maintenance of books and accounts
- Annual audit and annual accounts
- Security of property
- Keeping flat owners informed as to the management

It is also very important that all members of the flat management company have read and understood the lease as the lease will define the scope of landlord and leaseholder obligations. For example, repairing obligations are clearly outlined in leases and the policy of the landlord, and the ultimate strategy concerning repairs will need to be defined by the contents of the lease. Some leases will state that a landlord is responsible for all repairs to the structure and exterior of the property, including window frames and front doors. Other leases will limit that responsibility to the structure and exterior, excluding window frames. Ultimately, the policies and practice adopted by the management company will affect how much money is spent and by whom. To repeat, all policy of the management company must be formulated in accordance with the requirements of the lease and this must be clearly communicated to residents.

Insurance considerations

Insurance is normally collected through a service charge. The lease will, in nearly all cases, impose an insurance obligation on the landlord. The insurance will cover the main structure of the building and also public liability. As we have seen, leaseholders have the right to question insurance premiums. However, one advantage of being a shareholder in a company that owns the freehold is that you have complete control of the costs of insurance.

All leaseholders must be aware of the insurance policy, what it covers and how to claim in the event of an insurable loss. Likewise, the officer delegated to look after insurance must be fully acquainted with the nature of the policy and must be prepared to renegotiate the policy every year, ensuring value for money and the best possible cover.

Maintenance and repairs.

The management company, through the freeholders obligations in the lease, will have responsibility for the structure and exterior of the block. As we have seen, this will be more specifically defined in the lease. The management company will be responsible for the foundations of the block, external walls, roof and other supporting structures. In addition, any lifts or other machinery will be the responsibility of the company along with the general maintenance of the common parts. This will include boundary fences and drainage external to flats.

The management company will also be the 'responsible person' in relation to building safety and fire safety checks arising out of the 2021 legislation as discussed in chapter 1. These particular tasks, and planning for future payments is onerous.

The director dealing with maintenance will need to take on board the following:

- A full assessment of the company's liabilities for repair and maintenance will need to be undertaken through an analysis of the lease.
- This will need to be summarised and communicated to all leaseholders
- Quotations for work will need to be obtained before works are carried out. The director dealing with this will need to be fully acquainted with the provisions of Landlord and Tenant Acts as outlined earlier in this book. This is of fundamental importance. Remember, any money spent over a certain amount cannot be recovered unless the law has been adhered to. The important exception is emergencies.

The anticipation of future expenditure is very important in respect of future requirements. A decision has to be made as to whether leaseholders are charged as and when works are needed or whether a monthly "sinking fund" is levied, through the service charge, in order to cater for any future expenditure.

Remember that any money raised must be placed on an interest bearing account and placed in trust. Your bank can advise you on this aspect. The main point is to have some idea of requirements over the long term, say 25 years and to work out how much money will be needed to cater for this. This method of planning is infinitely more preferable to charging as and when repairs are needed, as money may not be available at this point and management problems may occur. Money paid into a sinking fund is not recoverable by individual leaseholders on sale as this payment is for wear and tear and belongs to the company.

Banking

Money needs to be collected from flat owners, either by standing order or direct debit and receipts issued. The director responsible for banking will usually hold the mandate for cheque signing, along with at least one other person.

Authorisation for signing cheques should never be vested in one person as this can lead to misappropriation of funds. The person dealing with banking will probably also be the person dealing with the overall treasury side of the business, including accounts and bookkeeping.

Rent and Service charge collection

This is usually delegated to one person. Without doubt, the best way to collect service charges and ground rent is through direct debit on a periodic basis, usually monthly. A healthy cash balance is always necessary in order to meet bills.

Preparation of annual budgets

Each year, an assessment of the likely expenditure for the forthcoming financial year will need to be undertaken. This will mean scrutinising the expenditure to date and assessing next year's expenditure on the basis of this. Where very heavy costs are anticipated, usually on an item of major repair, all leaseholders will need to be informed. As described above, if there is money in the pot to deal with it, life becomes that much easier than if all flat owners are to be billed.

One important point: short term thinking, resulting in short term savings for leaseholders is the very worst way of managing the economic process relating to property management. A monthly major repairs charge, through the service charge is, in the view of the author, absolutely necessary.

When it is prepared, the budget must be given to all

leaseholders (whether members of the company or not) and a clear month should be allowed for any feedback. In reality, with everyone so close to the process, then agreement can be reached before this time. When the budget has been accepted then a copy will need to be sent to all leaseholders, as the final copy and instructions given concerning the changing of direct debits.

If the management company is in the position of having no money to hand to carry out works and the billing of individual leaseholders is necessary then particular care should be taken to ensure that people are in receipt of clear advice concerning the amount for the work, their contribution, when it needs to be paid and how they can raise the money needed. It could be that advice needs to be given about loans, arrangements can be made to spread the payments over several years and so on. It really depends on the situation of the management company concerned.

Again, if you can avoid getting into this position through prudent management of charges, then life will be that much easier. A model service charge budget and accounts are shown at the end of the chapter.

Maintenance of accounting records

This function will be performed (preferably) by the same director who deals with other financial matters. In addition, the supervision of the preparation of annual accounts will be undertaken by the same person.

Security of property

This will normally be the responsibility of the person responsible for maintenance and repairs. Security will vary depending on the size and nature of the block of flats in question.

Keeping flat owners informed

Without doubt, one of the major problems in all organisations is that of communication, keeping others informed. If this can be achieved successfully then management becomes that much easier. One person will usually be appointed to do this.

Directors meetings

Directors of flat management companies should aim to have at least two formal meetings a year to review the operations of the company. Of course, meetings will be held informally at different times to discuss various issues. These should always be minuted. However, the six monthly meetings constitute formal meetings of directors. The company secretary will attend such meetings and will minute the proceedings and the minutes of the last meeting will need to be approved and signed as an accurate record. Some decisions may require a vote, which can be the majority of those present, with the chair holding a casting vote in cases of deadlock.

The chairman is usually appointed by the board to oversee the proceedings of the meetings.

Shareholders meetings

Meetings of the shareholders or members are known as general meetings. General meetings of a company is where the formal business of the company is conducted. All members of the company are entitled to attend and they are empowered to vote on certain matters. There are two types of meeting, the annual general meeting and the extraordinary general meeting.

The annual general meeting is where the directors of a company will subject themselves to the scrutiny of its members. It is necessary, by law, for a company to hold an AGM once every calendar year. The first AGM of a newly incorporated company will not be held until 18 months after incorporation.

Each subsequent AGM must happen not more than 15 months after the last one. Details concerning the nature, frequency and type of meeting can be obtained from companies house. The company secretary will call the AGM, the notice stating the following:

- A statement that the meeting is an AGM

- Details of the meeting, date, time and place
- An agenda of the business to be dealt with
- Details of the rights of members to appoint proxies to vote

This notice is served on all directors, members and auditors of the company. 21 days clear notice must be given of the AGM. If accounts are being presented at the meeting then copies have to be circulated with the notice. The usual business of an AGM is as follows:
- Election of officers
- Presentation of accounts
- Appointment of auditors
- Directors reports

Any other business should be allowed for at the end. Certain people may have grievances and it is good practice to allow these to be aired.

The articles of association will provide details of a necessary quorum in order to enable the meeting to proceed and decisions to be taken. Minutes must be kept and an annual return, which will normally be sent to the company will need to be submitted to companies house along with the accounts.

The meeting of members other than the AGM is known as

an extraordinary general meeting. This is hardly ever necessary. However, the facility for such a meeting does exist. The extraordinary general meeting would only be called in rare circumstances, such as the need to change an aspect of the running of the company which needs urgent agreement, this being the winding up of the company, a serious financial crisis and so on.

The company secretary will send a notice to members and can dispense with the notice period if necessary. The business at the EGM is transacted by the shareholders voting on whichever resolutions are proposed.

****

Model service charge/fire safety budget

ESTIMATE OF SERVICE CHARGES/FIRE SAFETY CHARGES-VICTORIA HOUSE, ALBERT ROAD, WALLINFORD. PERIOD 2021/2022

This estimate of charges has been prepared in accordance with the Landlord And Tenant Acts 1985 and 1987.

Period 5th April 2023 to 31st March 2024.

Charges   Current year charges

Charges 2020/2021

Cleaning of common parts

Gardening

Electricity

Gas

Insurance

Day to day maintenance

Major repairs fund

Cyclical maintenance

(Painting and decorating

at three yearly intervals)

FIRE SAFETY CHARGES (ESTIMATED)

FIRE ALARM MAINTENANCE

COMMISIONING AN EXTERNAL WALL SAFETY REPORT

CLADDING REMOVAL (IF NECESSARY)

       Total   Total

Number of flats

Charge per unit Per annum

        Per month

Your landlord is (Registered company)

Notes to above budget. It may be necessary to attach further notes with the budget for information purposes, particularly in the light of the new fire safety charges..

        ****

Model service charge accounts

(Registered company)

Expenditure statement for 5th April 2020 to 31st March 2021

Victoria House, Albert Road, Wallinford.

Service charge expenditure:

Cleaning of common parts

Gardening

Electricity

Gas

Insurance

Day to day maintenance

Major repairs fund

Cyclical maintenance

Total expenditure

Proportion payable in respect of

Less money paid on account

Balance due

Add ground rent for coming year
Any other

Note that this is a simple form of accounts for example only. It is highly likely that an accountant will prepare a form of accounts for leaseholders.

****

GLOSSARY OF TERMS

Assignment The transfer of a lease or tenancy from one person to another, usually by sale.

Blanket condition A term in a lease or tenancy that, if taken literally, would impose unreasonable constraints on the use of the premises.

Conveyance The transfer of a freehold from one person to another, usually by sale.

Determination A lease or tenancy is said to be determined when it is brought to an end by a positive act by either the landlord (freeholder) or tenant (leaseholder), as opposed to coming to an end because its term has expired. An outstanding example of a word used in one way by lawyers and another by everyone else.

Enfranchisement (individual) A lease is enfranchised when the leaseholder acquires the freehold. This has the effect of ending the lease and leaving the former leaseholder in sole possession of the freehold.

Enfranchisement (collective) The acquisition of the freehold on behalf of a number of leaseholders acting together.

Exclusive possession The right of a leaseholder or tenant to exclude other people, especially the landlord or freeholder, from the property.

Extension A lease is said to be extended when a longer term is agreed by both parties or (more usually) when it is replaced by a fresh lease with longer to run. The latter can happen either by agreement or as a result of the leaseholder exercising legal rights.

First-tier Tribunal The First Tier Tribunal handles applications, appeals and references relating to disputes over property and land.

Fixed term A fixed term tenancy or lease is one with a defined ending date, as opposed to a periodic tenancy.

Forfeiture The ultimate penalty if the leaseholder has breached the terms of the lease: the courts can end it and return the property to the freeholder.

Freeholder The owner of the strongest title to land available under English law. Freehold is tantamount to outright ownership and is treated as such in this book. The term 'freeholder' is used throughout to refer to the person granting the lease, although this will not always be the case in practice in practice - see the section on *Head leases and subleases* in Chapter 2.

Ground Rent A payment required under a lease, a source of income to the freeholder and a reminder to the leaseholder that he does not own the property outright.

Head lease When a leaseholder grants one or more subleases, the original lease is called the head lease.

Landlord The granter of a lease, tenancy, or licence.

Lease Strictly, the terms lease and tenancy are interchangeable. In this book, a lease is a tenancy with a fixed term of over seven years.

Leaseholder In this book, a tenant for a fixed term exceeding seven years.

Licence Permission to occupy land not amounting to a tenancy or lease, usually because exclusive possession is not granted.

Long lease Defined for various purposes under the 1967, 1987, and 1993 Acts as a lease originally granted for a fixed term of over 21 years.

Low rent A level of rent defined in the 1967, 1987, and 1993 Acts in ways that are intended to exclude the rent likely to be paid under a periodic tenancy or short fixed term tenancy.

Managing agent An organisation or (seldom) individual appointed by a freeholder to carry out some or all of his management responsibilities.

Management agreement Legal contract appointing a managing agent.

Management fee Payment due from the freeholder to the managing agent.

Marriage value Value by which the elements brought together by a lease enfranchisement, or extension, exceed their combined value as separate entities before it took place. The marriage value is sometimes a component in calculating the premium when leases are extended or enfranchised.

Mixed tenure A mixed tenure block is one that contains both leasehold and tenanted property.

Mortgagee The person or (usually) financial institution lending money against the security of property. Not to be confused with the following.

Mortgagor The owner of property, using it as security to raise a loan. 'Mortgagee' and 'mortgagor' are often confused, but if it is remembered that the owner of the property can be said to have mortgaged it, the difference becomes clear.

Nominee purchaser Whoever is chosen by the leaseholders involved in collective enfranchisement to be the new owner of the freehold: usually a company they have set up for the purpose.

Open market value The value of any saleable item assuming a willing seller and a willing buyer. The open market value of a freehold or a lease is a component in calculating the premium when leases are extended or enfranchised.

Period of grace Leases sold under the right to buy, and occasionally other leases, contain an estimate of future service charges, usually for the first five years of the lease. During this 'period of grace' any spending above the estimate cannot be recovered.

Periodic A periodic tenancy is one that runs from period to period (usually week to week or month to month) until something intervenes to stop it.

Pre-charging Charging for services in advance: used to build up a sinking fund.

Premium The payment due by the leaseholder to the freeholder when a lease is enfranchised or extended.

Qualifying leaseholders (or qualifying tenants) The tenants or leaseholders that qualify for the various rights, under the 1967, 1987, or 1993 Acts, to enfranchise or extend leases. The qualifications vary depending which right is being exercised under which Act.

Quiet enjoyment The right of leaseholders and tenants not to have their use of the property interfered with by the landlord: closely allied to exclusive possession.

Recognised tenants' association Body of leaseholders and/or tenants recognised by the freeholder for consultation purposes.

Re-entry Regaining possession of a property, for instance at the end of a tenancy or lease.

Rent Payment of (almost always) money in exchange for being allowed to occupy property under a lease, tenancy, or licence.

Residence test Requirement for most purposes under the 1967, 1987, and 1993 Acts that a leaseholder must live on the premises or have done so in the recent past. The exact test varies depending which right is being exercised.

Reversioner The person to whom possession will revert when the existing lease or tenancy comes to an end; usually the freeholder.

Right to buy A scheme, originally under the Housing Act 1980, allowing tenants of local authorities and some housing associations to buy their homes at a substantial discount.

Service charge Payment by leaseholders and tenants for services provided by the freeholder.

Shared ownership A scheme for assisted house purchase on part-buy, part-rent terms.

Sinking fund A fund built up on the service charge account by pre-charging.

Staircasing The purchase by a shared owner of an additional share of the property.

Sublease A lease granted by a leaseholder.

Tenant For the purpose of this book, someone holding a periodic tenancy or a tenancy granted for a fixed term of less than seven years.

Term The time for which a lease or fixed term tenancy will run.

****

Index

Accountants, 136
Accounts, 84
Annual audit, 139
Appointment of auditors, 147
Appointment of officers, 137
Articles of association, 136
Assignment, 56, 153

Building safety Act 2022, 9, 21
Building safety charges, 26, 27

Challenging Service Charges, 68, 85
Cladding, 24
Commonhold, 10, 35, 36, 37, 38, 46, 56, 57, 64, 66, 68, 76, 84, 85, 89
Commonhold and Leasehold Reform Act 2002, 38, 56
Consultation with Leaseholders, 76

Direct costs, 65, 66
Directors meetings, 145

Election of officers, 147
Enfranchisement, 153
Estimates, 78
Exclusive possession, 51
External wall system form (EWS1, 24

Fire Safety Act 2021, 9, 21, 47
Fire Safety Order 2005, 21
Flat management company, 134

Forfeiture, 57, 89, 154
Freehold, 35, 154

Good management, 53
Grant-aided works, 79
Grenfell Tower, 11, 22, 25

High Service Charges, 83, 89
Housing Act 1980, 39
Housing Act 1985, 67
Housing Act 1996, 46, 57, 68, 89

Insurance, 81, 138, 140, 151

Landlord and Tenant Act 1985, 46, 64, 66, 83, 84, 85, 87, 88, 123
Landlord and Tenant Act 1987, 6, 47, 52, 54, 66, 81, 123
Late charging, 80
Law of Property Act 1925, 58
Leasehold, 10, 35, 36, 37, 38, 46, 47, 54, 55, 57, 58, 64, 66, 68, 76, 84, 85, 87, 89
Leasehold Knowledge Partnership (LKP, 30
Leasehold Reform, Housing and Urban Development Act 1993, 38, 54, 55
Leasehold Valuation Tribunal, 55, 68, 87, 89
Leases, 36, 41, 47, 49, 56, 156

Maintenance and repairs, 138, 140
Major works, 77
Management fee, 65, 155
Memoranda, 136

Obligations of Freeholders, 51

Obligations of Leaseholders, 47

Presentation of accounts, 147

Quiet enjoyment, 51, 157

Recognised tenants' association, 55, 157
Rent and service charge collection, 139
Rent Assessment Committee, 83
Responsible Person, 22
Right to require information, 85

Service charges, 4, 63, 81, 84
Shared ownership, 40, 158
Shareholders meetings, 146
Subleases, 41

Tenancies, 36
The Buildings Safety Act 2022, 25
The Leasehold and Freehold Reform Act 2024, 3, 11, 18

Unpaid Service Charges, 89
Unreasonable Service Charges, 66

Valuation, 55, 68, 87, 89

Waking watch, 23
Waking Watch Relief Fund, 23

****

Useful addresses

The Property Institute (Formerly Association of Residential Managing Agents ARMA)
www.tpi.org.uk

Association of Retirement Housing Managers (ARHM)
1-3 Manor Road
Chatham
Kent
ME4 6AE
www.arhm.org

First Tier Tribunals (Property Chamber - Residential Property)
https://www.gov.uk/housing-tribunals/overview

Leasehold Advisory Service (LEASE)
Tel: 020 7832 2500
http://www.lease-advice.org

Leasehold Advice Centre
Lee House,
Northcote Lane,
Guildford,

Surrey GU5 0RB

01483 890672

www.leaseholdadvicecentre.co.uk

Leasehold Advisory Group (LAG)

Michael Tims and Co

80 Duke Street

Mayfair

London

W1K 6JG

0207 409 2233

www.michaeltims.co.uk

The Royal Institution of Chartered Surveyors (RICS)

London Office

12 Great George Street,

Parliament Square,

London SW1P 3AD

024 7686 8555

www.rics.org

RICS Birmingham Office

55 Colmore Row,

Birmingham, B3 2AA

024 7686 8555

RICS Scotland

3rd Floor,

125 Princes Street

Edinburgh

EH2 4AD

024 7686 8555

The Federation of Private Residents' Associations

PO Box 10271,

Epping,

CM16 9DB

01920 449839

Email: info@fpra.org.uk

www.fpra.org.uk

****

www.straightforwardbooks.co.uk

All titles, listed below, in the Straightforward Guides Series can be purchased (via Amazon) by going to www.straightforwardbooks.co.uk.

Law

A Straightforward Guide to:

Consumer Rights
Bankruptcy Insolvency and the Law
Employment Law
Healthcare Rights and law
A Simple Guide to Medical negligence
Private Tenants Rights
Family law
Small Claims in the County Court
Contract law
Intellectual Property and the law
Divorce and the law
Leaseholders Rights
The Process of Conveyancing
Knowing Your Rights and Using the Courts
Producing Your own Will
Housing Rights
The Bailiff the law and You
Probate and The Law
Company law

What to Expect When You Go to Court
Give me Your Money-Guide to Effective Debt Collection
Being a Litigant in Person
Conveyancing Residential property
A Practical Guide to Obtaining Probate
Marriage and Same Sex Partnerships
A Guide to Powers of Attorney
Mental Health and the Law
Criminal law

General titles, Including Emerald Guides

Letting Property for Profit
Buying, Selling and Renting property
Bookkeeping and Accounts for Small Business
Creative Writing
Freelance Writing
Writing Your own Life Story
Writing performance Poetry
Writing Romantic Fiction
Speech Writing
The Straightforward Business Plan
The Straightforward C.V.
Successful Public Speaking
Handling Bereavement
Individual and Personal Finance
The Crime Writers casebook
Being a Detective

A Comprehensive Guide to Arrest and Detention
A Comprehensive Guide to Burglary and Robbery
The Bailiff and You
Beating The Bully
Explaining Autism
Explaining Diabetes
Explaining Alzheimer's and Dementia
Explaining Asthma
Stop Smoking Now
Mind Power and Healthy Eating

Go to:

www.straightforwardbooks.co.uk